JANE EYRE
Stage 6

Jane Eyre begins life with all the disadvantages that nature and society can give her: she has no parents, no money, she is a girl (in a man's world), and, to make matters worse, she is not beautiful. She is made even more unattractive, in the eyes of the world, by having a strong character: she will not do what she is told to do.

She does not sound like the heroine of one of the great love stories of the world, and yet she behaves like one. The world looks at her, with all her disadvantages, and tells her to expect little from life. But Jane Eyre refuses to listen; she refuses to accept the unimportant place that the world offers to her. She demands that the world accept her as she is: not important, but the heroine of her own life; not beautiful, but deserving of love.

Charlotte Brontë (1816–55) is one of the great English novelists. Her own life, in Yorkshire in the north of England, was narrow and restricted, but her novels are justly famous for their passion and imagination.

OXFORD BOOKWORMS
Series Editor: Tricia Hedge

OXFORD BOOKWORMS

Stage 1 (400 words)

Love or Money? *Rowena Akinyemi*
One-Way Ticket *Jennifer Bassett*
  (short stories)
The President's Murderer *Jennifer Bassett*

*The Elephant Man *Tim Vicary*
White Death *Tim Vicary*
The Monkey's Paw *W.W.Jacobs*
Under the Moon *Rowena Akinyemi*

Stage 2 (700 words)

*Sherlock Holmes Short Stories
  Sir A. Conan Doyle
Voodoo Island *Michael Duckworth*
New Yorkers *O.Henry* (short stories)
The Death of Karen Silkwood
  Joyce Hannam

The Love of a King *Peter Dainty*
The Piano *Rosemary Border*
Grace Darling *Tim Vicary*
Dead Man's Island *John Escott*
Ear-rings from Frankfurt *Reg Wright*

Stage 3 (1000 words)

Go, Lovely Rose *H.E.Bates*
  (short stories)
The Picture of Dorian Gray
  Oscar Wilde
Chemical Secret *Tim Vicary*
Wyatt's Hurricane *Desmond Bagley*

Frankenstein *Mary Shelley*
*Skyjack! *Tim Vicary*
Love Story *Erich Segal*
Tooth and Claw *Saki* (short stories)
The Brontë Story *Tim Vicary*

Stage 4 (1400 words)

*The Hound of the Baskervilles
  Sir A. Conan Doyle
Three Men in a Boat *Jerome K. Jerome*
Mr Midshipman Hornblower *C.S.Forester*
Dr Jekyll and Mr Hyde *R.L.Stevenson*

Desert, Mountain, Sea *Sue Leather*
The Moonspinners *Mary Stewart*
Reflex *Dick Francis*
The Big Sleep *Raymond Chandler*
Death of an Englishman *Magdalen Nabb*

Stage 5 (1800 words)

*Ghost Stories *retold by Rosemary Border*
Heat and Dust *Ruth Prawer Jhabvala*
This Rough Magic *Mary Stewart*
Wuthering Heights *Emily Brontë*
Far from the Madding Crowd
  Thomas Hardy

The Bride Price *Buchi Emecheta*
The Dead of Jericho *Colin Dexter*
Great Expectations *Charles Dickens*
I, Robot *Isaac Asimov*
Brat Farrar *Josephine Tey*

Stage 6 (2500 words)

*Tess of the d'Urbervilles *Thomas Hardy*
Meteor *John Wyndham* (short stories)
Night Without End *Alistair MacLean*
Oliver Twist *Charles Dickens*

Cry Freedom *John Briley*
Jane Eyre *Charlotte Brontë*
The Enemy *Desmond Bagley*
Deadheads *Reginald Hill*

Cassettes available for these titles
For a current list of titles, please refer to the Oxford English *catalogue.*

Jane Eyre

Charlotte Brontë

retold by
Clare West

OXFORD UNIVERSITY PRESS

Oxford University Press
Walton Street, Oxford OX2 6DP

Oxford New York Toronto Madrid
Delhi Bombay Calcutta Madras Karachi
Kuala Lumpur Singapore Hong Kong Tokyo
Nairobi Dar es Salaam Cape Town
Melbourne Auckland
and associated companies in
Berlin Ibadan

OXFORD and OXFORD ENGLISH
are trade marks of Oxford University Press

ISBN 0 19 421632 2

This simplified edition
© Oxford University Press 1990

First published 1990
Third impression 1992

All rights reserved. No part of this publication may
be reproduced, stored in a retrieval system, or transmitted,
in any form or by any means, electronic, mechanical,
photocopying, recording, or otherwise, without the prior
permission of Oxford University Press.

This book is sold subject to the condition that it shall not,
by way of trade or otherwise, be lent, re-sold, hired out, or
otherwise circulated without the publisher's prior consent
in any form of binding or cover other than that in which it is
published and without a similar condition including this
condition being imposed on the subsequent purchaser.

The publishers would like to thank the following
for their permission to reproduce illustrations:
The Ronald Grant Collection, The Kobal Collection

The publishers have made every effort to contact the
copyright holder of the cover photograph, but have been unable
to do so. If the copyright holder would like to contact the
publishers, the publishers would be happy to pay an
appropriate reproduction fee.

Typeset by Pentacor PLC, High Wycombe, Bucks
Printed in England by Clays Ltd, St Ives plc

People in this Story

Jane Eyre

At Gateshead
Mrs Reed, Jane Eyre's aunt
Eliza Reed   )
Georgiana Reed   ) Jane Eyre's cousins
John Reed   )
Bessie, the nursemaid
Miss Abbott, Mrs Reed's maid
Dr Lloyd
Robert, the coachman

At Lowood School
Mr Brocklehurst, the school's financial manager
Miss Temple, the headmistress
Miss Miller   )
Miss Scatcherd   )teachers
Helen Burns, a pupil

At Thornfield
Mrs Fairfax, the housekeeper
Adèle, daughter of Mr Rochester's French mistress
Edward Rochester, the owner of Thornfield Hall
Blanche Ingram   )
Mary Ingram   )sisters
Lady Ingram, their mother
Grace Poole
Dick Mason
Mr Briggs, lawyer to Mr Eyre of Madeira
Bertha Mason

At Moor House
Diana Rivers   )
Mary Rivers   )sisters
St John Rivers, brother of Diana and Mary, and vicar of Morton
Hannah, his housekeeper
Rosamund Oliver, daughter of a rich factory-owner

At Ferndean Manor
John   )
Mary, his wife   )Mr Rochester's servants

Part One – A child at Gateshead

1

The red room

We could not go for a walk that afternoon. There was such a freezing cold wind, and such heavy rain, that we all stayed indoors. I was glad of it. I never liked long walks, especially in winter. I used to hate coming home when it was almost dark, with ice-cold fingers and toes, feeling miserable because Bessie, the nursemaid, was always scolding me. All the time I knew I was different from my cousins, Eliza, John and Georgiana Reed. They were taller and stronger than me, and they were loved.

These three usually spent their time crying and quarrelling, but today they were sitting quietly around their mother in the sitting-room. I wanted to join the family circle, but Mrs Reed, my aunt, refused. Bessie had complained about me.

'No, I'm sorry, Jane. Until I hear from Bessie, or see for myself, that you are really trying to behave better, you cannot be treated as a good, happy child, like *my* children.'

'What does Bessie say I have done?' I asked.

'Jane, it is not polite to question me in that way. If you cannot speak pleasantly, be quiet.'

I crept out of the sitting-room and into the small room next door, where I chose a book full of pictures from the bookcase. I climbed on to the window-seat and drew the curtains, so that I was completely hidden. I sat there for a while. Sometimes I looked out of the window at the grey November afternoon, and saw the rain pouring down on the leafless garden. But most of the time I studied the book and stared, fascinated, at the pictures. Lost in the world of imagination, I forgot my sad, lonely existence for a while, and was happy. I was only afraid that my secret hiding-place might be discovered.

Suddenly the door of the room opened. John Reed rushed in.

'Where are you, rat?' he shouted. He did not see me behind the curtain. 'Eliza! Georgy! Jane isn't here! Tell Mamma she's run out into the rain – what a bad animal she is!'

'How lucky I drew the curtain,' I thought. He would never have found me, because he was not very intelligent. But Eliza guessed at once where I was.

'She's in the window-seat, John,' she called from the sitting-room. So I came out immediately, as I did not want him to pull me out.

'What do you want?' I asked him.

'Say, "What do you want, *Master* Reed",' he answered, sitting in an armchair. 'I want you to come here.'

John Reed was fourteen and I was only ten. He was large and rather fat. He usually ate too much at meals, which made him ill. He should have been at boarding school, but his mother, who loved him very much, had brought him home for a month or two, because she thought his health was delicate.

John did not love his mother or his sisters, and he hated me. He bullied and punished me, not two or three times a week, not once or twice a day, but all the time. My whole body trembled when he came near. Sometimes he hit me, sometimes he just threatened me, and I lived in terrible fear of him. I had no idea how to stop him. The servants did not want to offend their young master, and Mrs Reed could see no fault in her dear boy.

So I obeyed John's order and approached his armchair, thinking how very ugly his face was. Perhaps he understood what I was thinking, for he hit me hard on the face.

'That is for your rudeness to Mamma just now,' he said, 'and for your wickedness in hiding, and for looking at me like that, you rat!'

I was so used to his bullying that I never thought of hitting him back.

'What were you doing behind that curtain?' he asked.

'I was reading,' I answered.

'Show me the book.' I gave it to him.

'You have no right to take our books,' he continued. 'You have no money and your father left you none. You ought to beg in the streets, not live here in comfort with a gentleman's family. Anyway, all these books are mine, and so is the whole house, or will be in a few years' time. I'll teach you not to borrow my books again.' He lifted the heavy book and threw it hard at me.

It hit me and I fell, cutting my head on the door. I was in great pain, and suddenly for the first time in my life, I forgot my fear of John Reed.

'You wicked, cruel boy!' I cried. 'You are a bully! You are as bad as a murderer!'

'What! What!' he cried. 'Did she say that to me? Did you hear, Eliza and Georgiana? I'll tell Mamma, but first . . .'

He rushed to attack me, but now he was fighting with a desperate girl. I really saw him as a wicked murderer. I felt the blood running down my face, and the pain gave me strength. I fought back as hard as I could. My resistance surprised him, and he shouted for help. His sisters ran for Mrs Reed, who called her maid, Miss Abbott, and Bessie. They pulled us apart and I heard them say, 'What a wicked girl! She attacked Master John!'

Mrs Reed said calmly, 'Take her away to the red room and lock her in there.' And so I was carried upstairs, arms waving and legs kicking.

As soon as we arrived in the red room, I became quiet again, and the two servants both started scolding me.

'Really, Miss Eyre,' said Miss Abbott, 'how could you hit him? He's your young master!'

'How can he be my master? I am not a servant!' I cried.

'No, Miss Eyre, you are less than a servant, because you do not work,' replied Miss Abbott. They both looked at me as if they strongly disapproved of me.

'You should remember, miss,' said Bessie, 'that your aunt pays for your food and clothes, and you should be grateful. You have no other relations or friends.'

All my short life I had been told this, and I had no answer to it. I stayed silent, listening to these painful reminders.

'And if you are angry and rude, Mrs Reed may send you away,' added Bessie.

'Anyway,' said Miss Abbott, 'God will punish you, Jane Eyre, for your wicked heart. Pray to God, and say you're sorry.' They left the room, locking the door carefully behind them.

The red room was a cold, silent room, hardly ever used, although it was one of the largest bedrooms in the house. Nine years ago my uncle, Mr Reed, had died in this room, and since then nobody had wanted to sleep in it.

Now that I was alone I thought bitterly of the people I lived with. John Reed, his sisters, his mother, the servants – they all accused me, scolded me, hated me. Why could I never please them? Eliza was selfish, but was respected. Georgiana had a bad temper, but she was popular with everybody because she was beautiful. John was rude, cruel and violent, but nobody punished him. I tried to make no mistakes, but they called me naughty every moment of the day. Now that I had turned against John to protect myself, everybody blamed me.

And so I spent that whole long afternoon in the red room asking myself why I had to suffer and why life was so unfair. Perhaps I would run away, or starve myself to death.

Gradually it became dark outside. The rain was still beating on the windows, and I could hear the wind in the trees. Now I was no longer angry, and I began to think the Reeds might be right. Perhaps

I *was* wicked. Did I deserve to die, and be buried in the churchyard like my uncle Reed? I could not remember him, but knew he was my mother's brother, who had taken me to his house when my parents both died. On his death bed he had made his wife, aunt Reed, promise to look after me like her own children. I supposed she now regretted her promise.

A strange idea came to me. I felt sure that if Mr Reed had lived he would have treated me kindly, and now, as I looked round at the dark furniture and the walls in shadow, I began to fear that his ghost might come back to punish his wife for not keeping her promise. He might rise from the grave in the churchyard and appear in this room! I was so frightened by this thought that I hardly dared to breathe. Suddenly in the darkness I saw a light moving on the ceiling. It may have been from a lamp outside, but in my nervous state I did not think of that. I felt sure it must be a ghost, a visitor from another world. My head was hot, my heart beat fast. Was that the sound of wings in my ears? Was that something moving near me? Screaming wildly, I rushed to the door and shook it. Miss Abbott and Bessie came running to open it.

'Miss Eyre, are you ill?' asked Bessie.

'Take me out of here!' I screamed.

'Why? What's the matter?' she asked.

'I saw a light, and I thought it was a ghost,' I cried, holding tightly on to Bessie's hand.

'She's not even hurt,' said Miss Abbott in disgust. 'She screamed just to bring us here. I know all her little tricks.'

'What is all this?' demanded an angry voice. Mrs Reed appeared at the door of the room. 'Abbott and Bessie, I think I told you to leave Jane Eyre in this room till I came.'

'She screamed so loudly, ma'am,' said Bessie softly.

'Let go of her hands, Bessie,' was Mrs Reed's only answer. 'Jane Eyre, you need not think you can succeed in getting out of the room like this. Your naughty tricks will not work with me. You will stay here an hour longer as a punishment for trying to deceive us.'

'Oh aunt, please forgive me! I can't bear it! I shall die if you keep me here . . .' I screamed and kicked as she held me.

'Silence! Control yourself!' She pushed me, resisting wildly, back into the red room and locked me in. There I was in the darkness again, with the silence and the ghosts. I must have fainted. I cannot remember anything more.

2

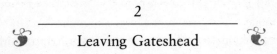

Leaving Gateshead

I woke up to find the doctor lifting me very carefully into my own bed. It was good to be back in my familiar bedroom, with a warm fire and candle-light. It was also a great relief to recognize Dr Lloyd, who Mrs Reed called in for her servants (she always called a specialist for herself and the children). He was looking after me so kindly. I felt he would protect me from Mrs Reed. He talked to me a little, then gave Bessie orders to take good care of me. When he left, I felt very lonely again.

But I was surprised to find that Bessie did not scold me at all. In fact she was so kind to me that I became brave enough to ask a question.

'Bessie, what's happened? Am I ill?'

'Yes, you became ill in the red room, but you'll get better, don't worry, Miss Jane,' she answered. Then she went next door to fetch another servant. I could hear her whispers.

'Sarah, come in here and sleep with me and that poor child tonight. I daren't stay alone with her, she might die. She was so ill last night! Do you think she saw a ghost? Mrs Reed was too hard on her, I think.' So the two servants slept in my room, while I lay awake all night, trembling with fear, and eyes wide open in horror, imagining ghosts in every corner.

Fortunately I suffered no serious illness as a result of my terrible experience in the red room, although I shall never forget that night. But the shock left me nervous and depressed for the next few days. I cried all day long and although Bessie tried hard to tempt me with nice things to eat or my favourite books, I took no pleasure in eating or even in reading. I knew I had no one to love me and nothing to look forward to.

When the doctor came again, he seemed a little surprised to find me looking so miserable.

'Perhaps she's crying because she couldn't go out with Mrs Reed in the carriage this morning,' suggested Bessie.

'Surely she's more sensible than that,' said the doctor, smiling at me. 'She's a big girl now.'

'I'm not crying about that. I hate going out in the carriage,' I said quickly. 'I'm crying because I'm miserable.'

'Oh really, Miss!' said Bessie.

The doctor looked at me thoughtfully. He had small, grey, intelligent eyes. Just then a bell rang for the servants' dinner.

'You can go, Bessie,' he said. 'I'll stay here talking to Miss Jane till you come back.'

After Bessie had left, he asked, 'What really made you ill?'

'I was locked up in a room with a ghost, in the dark.'

'Afraid of ghosts, are you?' he smiled.

'Of Mr Reed's ghost, yes. He died in that room, you know. Nobody even goes in there any more. It was cruel to lock me in there alone without a candle. I shall never forget it!'

'But you aren't afraid now. There must be another reason why you are so sad,' he said, looking kindly at me.

How could I tell him all the reasons for my unhappiness!

'I have no father or mother, brothers or sisters,' I began.

'But you have a kind aunt and cousins.'

'But John Reed knocked me down and my aunt locked me in the red room,' I cried. There was a pause.

'Don't you like living at Gateshead, in such a beautiful house?' he asked.

'I would be glad to leave it, but I have nowhere else to go.'

'You have no relations apart from Mrs Reed?'

'I think I may have some, who are very poor, but I know nothing about them,' I answered.

'Would you like to go to school?' he asked finally. I thought for a moment. I knew very little about school, but at least it would be a change, the start of a new life.

'Yes, I *would* like to go,' I replied in the end.

'Well, well,' said the doctor to himself as he got up, 'we'll see. The child is delicate, she ought to have a change of air.'

I heard later from the servants that he had spoken to Mrs Reed about me, and that she had agreed immediately to send me to school. Abbott said Mrs Reed would be glad to get rid of me. In this conversation I also learned for the first time that my father had been a poor vicar. When he married my mother, Miss Jane Reed of Gateshead, the Reed family were so angry that they disinherited her. I also heard that my parents both died of an illness only a year after their wedding.

But days and weeks passed, and Mrs Reed still said nothing about sending me to school. One day, as she was scolding me, I suddenly threw a question at her. The words just came out without my planning to say them.

'What would uncle Reed say to you if he were alive?' I asked.

'What?' cried Mrs Reed, her cold grey eyes full of fear, staring at me as if I were a ghost. I had to continue.

'My uncle Reed is now in heaven, and can see all you think and do, and so can my parents. They know how you hate me, and are cruel to me.'

Mrs Reed smacked my face and left me without a word. I was scolded for an hour by Bessie as the most ungrateful child in the world, and indeed with so much hate in my heart I did feel wicked.

Christmas passed by, with no presents or new clothes for me. Every evening I watched Eliza and Georgiana putting on their new dresses and going out to parties. Sometimes Bessie would come up to me in my lonely bedroom, bringing a piece of cake, sometimes she would tell me a story, and sometimes she would kiss me good night. When she was kind to me I thought she was the best person in the world, but she did not always have time for me.

On the morning of the fifteenth of January, Bessie rushed up to my room, to tell me a visitor wanted to see me. Who could it be? I knew Mrs Reed would be there too and I was frightened of seeing her again. When I nervously entered the breakfast-room I looked up at – a black column! At least that is what he looked like to me. He was a tall, thin man dressed all in black, with a cold, stony face at the top of the column.

'This is the little girl I wrote to you about,' said Mrs Reed to the stony stranger.

'Well, Jane Eyre,' said the stranger heavily, 'and are you a good child?'

It was impossible to say yes, with Mrs Reed sitting there, so I was silent.

'Perhaps the less said about that, the better, Mr Brocklehurst,' said Mrs Reed, shaking her head.

'I'm sorry to hear it,' he answered. 'Come here, Jane Eyre, and answer my questions. Where do the wicked go after death?'

'They go to hell,' I answered.

'And what must you do to avoid going there?' he asked.

I thought for a moment, but could not find the right answer.

'I must keep in good health, and not die,' I replied.

'Wrong! Children younger than you die all the time. Another question. Do you enjoy reading the Bible?'

'Yes, sometimes,' I replied, hesitating.

'That is not enough. Your answers show me you have a wicked heart. You must pray to God to change it, if you ever want to go to heaven.'

'Mr Brocklehurst,' interrupted Mrs Reed, 'I mentioned to you in my letter that this little girl has in fact a very bad character. If you accept her at Lowood school, please make sure that the headmistress and teachers know how dishonest she is. She will try to lie to them of course. You see, Jane, you cannot try your tricks on Mr Brocklehurst.'

However hard I had tried to please Mrs Reed in the past, she always thought the worst of me. It was not surprising that I had come to hate her. Now she was accusing me in front of a stranger. My hopes of starting a new life at school began to fade.

'Do not worry, madam,' Mr Brocklehurst said, 'the teachers will watch her carefully. Life at Lowood will do her good. We believe in hard work, plain food, simple clothes and no luxury of any kind.'

'I will send her as soon as possible then, Mr Brocklehurst. I hope she will be taught according to her low position in life.'

'Indeed she will, madam. I hope she will be grateful for this opportunity to improve her character. Little girl, read this book. It tells the story of the sudden death of a young girl who was a liar. Read and pray.'

After Mr Brocklehurst had given me the book and left, I felt I had to speak. Anger was boiling up inside me. I walked up to Mrs Reed and looked straight into her eyes.

'I do *not* deceive people! If I told lies, I would say I loved you! But I don't, I hate you! I will never call you aunt again as long as I live. If anyone asks how you treated me, I will tell them the truth, that you were very cruel to me. People think you are a good woman, but *you* are lying to *them*!'

Even before I had finished I began to experience a great feeling of freedom and relief. At last I had said what I felt! Mrs Reed looked frightened and unhappy.

'Jane, I want to be your friend. You don't know what you're saying. You are too excited. Go to your room and lie down.'

'I won't lie down. I'm quite calm. Send me to school soon, Mrs Reed. I hate living here.'

'I will indeed send her soon,' murmured Mrs Reed to herself.

Part Two — A girl at Lowood

3

 My first impressions of school

Mrs Reed arranged for me to leave on the nineteenth of January. I had to get up very early to catch the coach, but Bessie helped me to get ready.

'Will you say goodbye to Mrs Reed, Jane?' she asked.

'No, she said I shouldn't disturb her so early. Anyway, I don't want to say anything to her. She's always hated me.'

'Oh, Miss Jane, don't say that!'

'Goodbye to Gateshead!' I shouted wildly, as we walked together out of the front door, to wait for the coach in the road. It arrived, pulled by four horses, and full of passengers. The coachman took my luggage and called me to hurry up. Bessie kissed me for the last time as I held tightly to her.

She shouted up to the coachman, 'Make sure you take care of her! Fifty miles is a long way for a young child to go alone.'

'I will!' he answered. The door was closed, and the coach rolled off. What a strange feeling to be leaving Gateshead, my home for the whole of my childhood! Although I was sad to say goodbye to Bessie, I was both excited and nervous about the new places I would see, and the new people I would meet.

I do not remember much about the journey, except that it seemed far too long. We stopped for lunch, to change the horses. Then in the afternoon I realized we were driving through countryside. I slept for a short time but was woken when the coach stopped. The door opened and a servant called in,

'Is there a little girl called Jane Eyre here?'

'Yes,' I answered, and was helped out of the coach with my

luggage. Tired and confused after the journey, I followed the servant into a large building, where she left me in a sitting-room. In came a tall lady, with dark hair and eyes, and a large, pale forehead. I discovered that she was Miss Temple, the headmistress of Lowood school. She looked at me carefully.

'You are very young to be sent alone. You look tired. Are you?' she asked, putting her hand kindly on my shoulder.

'A little, ma'am,' I replied.

'How old are you, and what is your name?'

'I'm Jane Eyre, ma'am, and I'm ten years old.'

'Well, I hope you will be a good child at school,' she said, touching my cheek gently with her finger.

I was taken by a teacher, Miss Miller, through the silent corridors of the large school, to the long, wide schoolroom. There about eighty girls, aged from nine to twenty, sat doing their homework. I sat on a bench near the door, with my slate.

'Put away the lesson-books and fetch the supper-trays!' called Miss Miller. Four tall girls removed all the books, then went out and returned with trays which were handed round. Each child could have a drink of water out of the shared cup, and could take a small piece of biscuit. Then we all went quietly upstairs to the long, crowded bedroom, where two children shared every bed. I had to share Miss Miller's, but I was so tired that I fell asleep immediately.

In the morning the ringing of a bell woke me, although it was still dark. I got dressed quickly in the bitter cold of the room, and washed when I could. There was only one basin for six girls. When the bell rang again, we all went downstairs, two by two, and silently entered the cold, badly lit schoolroom for prayers. As the bell rang a third time to indicate the beginning of lessons, the girls moved into four groups around four tables, and the teachers came into the room to start the Bible class. I was put in the bottom class. How glad I was when it was time for breakfast! I had hardly eaten anything the day before. But the only food served to us was porridge, which was burnt. It was so disgusting that we could not eat it, so we left the dining-room with empty stomachs. After breakfast came the one happy moment of the day, when the pupils could play and talk freely. We all complained bitterly about the uneatable breakfast. Lessons started again at nine o'clock and finished at twelve, when Miss Temple stood up to speak to the whole school.

'Girls, this morning you had a breakfast which you couldn't eat. You must be hungry, so I have ordered a lunch of bread and cheese for you all.' The teachers looked at her in surprise.

'Don't worry, I take responsibility for it,' she told them.

We were delighted, and all rushed out into the garden to eat our lunch. Nobody had taken any notice of me so far, but I did not mind that. I stood alone outside, watching some of the stronger girls playing, trying to forget the bitter cold, and thinking about my life. Gateshead and the Reed family seemed a long way away. I was not yet used to school life. And what sort of future could I look forward to?

As I wondered, I saw a girl near me reading a book. I felt brave enough to speak to her, since I too liked reading.

'Is your book interesting? What is it about?' I asked.

'Well, *I* like it,' she said after a pause, looking at me. 'Here, have a look at it.' I glanced quickly at it but found it too difficult to understand, so I gave it back.

'What sort of school is this?' I asked.

'It's called Lowood school. It's a charity school. We're all charity children, you see. I expect your parents are dead, aren't they? All the girls here have lost either one or both parents.'

'Don't we pay anything? Is the school free?' I asked.

'We pay, or our relations pay, £15 a year for each of us. That isn't enough, so some kind ladies and gentlemen in London pay the rest. That's why it's called a charity school.'

'Who is Mr Brocklehurst?' was my next question.

'His mother built this part of the school. He's the manager, and looks after all financial matters. He lives in a large house near here.'

I did not see her again until during the afternoon lessons, when I noticed that she had been sent to stand alone in the middle of the schoolroom. I could not imagine what she had done to deserve such a punishment, but she did not look ashamed or unhappy. She was lost in thought, and did not seem to notice that everyone was looking at her.

'If that happened to me,' I thought, 'I would be so embarrassed!'

After lessons we had a small cup of coffee and half a piece of brown bread, then half an hour's play, then homework. Finally, after the evening biscuit and drink of water, we said prayers and went to bed. That was my first day at Lowood.

4

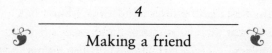

Making a friend

*T*he next morning we got up in the dark as before, but the water was frozen, so we could not wash. It was freezing cold in all the rooms. This time the porridge was not burnt, but I still felt hungry, as the quantity was so small.

I stayed in the bottom class, but noticed the girl that I had been talking to was in another class. Her surname seemed to be Burns. Teachers called girls by their surnames in this school. Her class were studying history, and her teacher, Miss Scatcherd, appeared constantly annoyed by her.

'Burns, hold your head up, can't you!'

'Burns, don't stand like that!'

The history questions asked by Miss Scatcherd sounded very difficult, but Burns knew all the answers. I kept expecting the teacher to praise her, but instead she suddenly cried out,

'You dirty girl! You haven't washed your hands this morning!'

I was surprised that Burns did not explain that none of us could wash our faces or hands because the water had been frozen. Miss Scatcherd gave an order. Burns left the room and returned, carrying a stick. The teacher took it and hit Burns several times with it. The girl did not cry or change her expression.

'Wicked girl!' said Miss Scatcherd. 'Nothing will change your dirty habits!'

Later that day, during the play-hour, I found Burns alone by the fireside, reading the same book as before, and I started talking to her.

'What is the rest of your name?' I asked.

'Helen,' she replied.

'Do you want to leave Lowood?'

'No, why should I? I was sent to school here, so I must learn as much as I can.'

'But Miss Scatcherd is so cruel to you!' I burst out.

'Cruel? Not at all. She is strict and she sees my faults.'

'If I were you, I'd hate her,' I cried. 'If she hit me with a stick, I'd seize it and break it under her nose.'

'I don't think you would,' answered Helen quietly. 'And if you did, Mr Brocklehurst would send you away from school, and your relations would be upset. Anyway, the Bible tells us to do good, even if other people hurt us. Sometimes you have to put up with some hard things in life.'

I could not understand her ideas but I had a feeling she might be right. I looked at her in wonder.

'You say you have faults, Helen. What are they? To me you seem very good.'

'You are wrong,' she answered. 'I'm untidy and careless and I forget the rules. I read when I should be doing my homework. You see, Miss Scatcherd is right to scold me.'

'Is Miss Temple as strict as that?' I asked.

A soft smile passed over Helen's normally serious face.

'Miss Temple is full of goodness. She gently tells me of my mistakes, and praises me if I do well. But even with her help I don't concentrate properly in class, I just dream away the time, and then I can't answer the teacher's questions.'

'But today in history you knew all the answers!' I said.

'I just happened to be interested, that's all,' she replied.

'I expect you are always interested in Miss Temple's lessons, because you like her and she is good to you. I'm like that. I love those who love me, and I hate those who punish me unfairly.'

'You should read the Bible and do what Christ says – people who believe in God should love their enemies,' said Helen.

'Then I should love Mrs Reed and her son John, which is impossible,' I cried.

Helen asked me to explain what I meant, and listened carefully to the long story of what I had suffered at Gateshead.

'Well,' I asked impatiently at the end, 'isn't Mrs Reed a bad woman? Don't you agree with me?'

'It's true she has been unkind to you, because she dislikes your faults, as Miss Scatcherd dislikes mine. But look how bitterly you remember every angry word! Wouldn't you be happier if you tried to forget her scolding? Life is too short to continue hating anyone for a long time. We all have faults, but the time will come soon when we die, when our wickedness will pass away with our bodies, leaving only the pure flame of the spirit. That's why I never think of revenge, I never consider life unfair. I live in calm, looking forward to the end.'

For a moment we both stayed silent. Then one of the big girls came up, calling, 'Helen Burns! Go and put away your work and tidy your drawer immediately, or I'll tell Miss Scatcherd!'

Helen sighed, and, getting up, silently obeyed.

5

Mr Brocklehurst's visit
and its results

*I*t was difficult for me to get used to the school rules at Lowood, and to the hard physical conditions. In January, February and March there was deep snow, but we still had to spend an hour outside every day. We had no boots or gloves, and my hands and feet ached badly. We were growing children, and needed more food than was provided. Sometimes the big girls bullied us little ones and made us hand over our teatime bread or evening biscuit.

One afternoon, when I had been at Lowood for three weeks, a visitor arrived. All the teachers and pupils stood respectfully as he entered the schoolroom. I looked up. There, next to Miss Temple, stood the same black column which had frowned on me in the breakfast-room at Gateshead. I had been afraid he would come. I remembered only too well Mrs Reed's description of my character, and the promise he had given her to warn teachers at Lowood about my wickedness. Now they would consider me a bad child for ever.

At first Mr Brocklehurst spoke in a murmur to Miss Temple. I could just hear because I was at the front of the class.

'Tell the housekeeper she must count the needles, and only give out one at a time to the girls – they lose them so easily! And Miss Temple, please make sure the girls' stockings are mended more carefully. Some of them have a lot of holes.'

'I shall follow your instructions, sir,' said Miss Temple.

'And another thing which surprises me, I find that a lunch of bread and cheese has been served to the girls recently. Why is this? There is nothing about it in the rules! Who is responsible?'

'I myself, sir,' answered Miss Temple. 'The breakfast was so badly cooked that the girls couldn't possibly eat it, so they were hungry.'

'Madam, listen to me for a moment. You know that I am trying to bring up these girls to be strong, patient and unselfish. If some little luxury is not available, do not replace it with something else, but tell them to be brave and suffer, like Christ Himself. Remember what the Bible says, man shall not live by bread alone, but by the word of God! Madam, when you put bread into these children's mouths, you feed their bodies but you starve their souls!'

Miss Temple did not reply. She looked straight in front of her, and her face was as cold and hard as marble. Mr Brocklehurst, on the other hand, now looked round at the girls, and almost jumped in surprise.

'Who – what is that girl with red hair, with *curls*, madam, with curls everywhere?'

'That is Julia Severn,' said Miss Temple quietly. 'Her hair curls naturally, you see.'

'Naturally! Yes, but it is God we obey, not nature! Miss Temple, that girl's hair must be cut off. I have said again and again that hair must be arranged modestly and plainly. I see other girls here with too much hair. Yes, I shall send someone tomorrow to cut all the girls' hair.'

'Mr Brocklehurst . . .' began Miss Temple.

'No, Miss Temple, I insist. To please God these girls must have short, straight hair and plain, simple clothes . . .'

He was interrupted by the arrival of three ladies, who had unfortunately not heard his comments on dress and hair. They all wore the most expensive clothes and had beautiful, long, curly hair. I heard Miss Temple greet them as the wife and daughters of Mr Brocklehurst.

I had hoped to hide my face behind my slate while Mr Brocklehurst was talking, so that he would not recognize me, but suddenly the slate fell from my hand and broke in two on the hard floor. I knew only too well what would happen next.

'A careless girl!' said Mr Brocklehurst quietly, almost to himself.

'The new girl, I see. I must not forget to say something to the whole school about her.' And then to me, aloud,

'Come here, child.'

I was too frightened to move, but two big girls pushed me towards him. Miss Temple whispered kindly in my ear,

'Don't be afraid, Jane. I saw it was an accident.' Her kindness touched me, but I knew that soon she would hear the lies about me, and then she would hate me!

'Put the child on that chair,' said Mr Brocklehurst. Someone lifted me up on to a high chair, so that I was close to his nose. Frightened and shaking, I felt everyone's eyes on me.

Frightened and shaking, I felt everyone's eyes on me.

'You see this girl?' began the black marble column. 'She is young, she looks like an ordinary child. Nothing about her tells you she is evil. But she is all wickedness! Children, don't talk to her, stay away from her. Teachers, watch her, punish her body to save her soul – if indeed she has a soul, because this child . . . I can hardly say it . . . this child is a liar!'

'How shocking!' said the two Brocklehurst daughters, each wiping a tear or two from their eyes.

'I learned this fact,' continued the great man, 'from Mrs Reed, the kind lady who took care of her after her parents' death and brought her up as a member of the family. In the end Mrs Reed was so afraid of this child's evil influence on her own children that she had to send her here. Teachers, watch her carefully!'

The Brocklehurst family stood up and moved slowly out of the schoolroom. At the door, my judge turned and said,

'She must stand half an hour longer on that chair, and nobody may speak to her for the rest of the day.'

So there I was, high up on the chair, publicly displayed as an ugly example of evil. Feelings of shame and anger boiled up inside me, but just as I felt I could not bear it any longer, Helen Burns walked past me and lifted her eyes to mine. Her look calmed me. What a smile she had! It was an intelligent, brave smile, lighting up her thin face and her tired grey eyes.

When all the girls left the schoolroom at five o'clock, I climbed down from the chair and sat on the floor. I no longer felt strong or calm, and I began to cry bitterly. I had wanted so much to make friends at Lowood, to be good, to deserve praise. Now nobody would believe me or perhaps even speak to me. Could I ever start a new life after this?

'Never!' I cried. 'I wish I were dead!' Just then Helen arrived, bringing my coffee and bread. I was too upset to eat or drink, but she sat with me for some time, talking gently to me, wiping away my tears, and helping me to recover. When Miss Temple came to look for me, she found us sitting quietly together.

'Come up to my room, both of you,' she said.

We went to her warm, comfortable room upstairs.

'Now tell me the truth, Jane,' she said. 'You have been accused, and you must have the chance to defend yourself.'

And so I told her the whole story of my lonely childhood with the Reed family, and of my terrible experience in the red room.

'I know Dr Lloyd, who saw you when you were ill,' she said. 'I'll write to him and see if he agrees with what you say. If he does, I shall publicly tell the school you are not a liar. *I* believe you *now*, Jane.' And she kissed me. She turned to Helen.

'How are you tonight, Helen? Have you coughed a lot today?'

'Not very much, ma'am.'

'And the pain in your chest?'

'It's a little better, I think.'

Miss Temple examined Helen carefully, and sighed a little. Then she gave us some tea and toast. For a while I felt I was in heaven, eating and drinking in the warm, pretty room, with kind Miss Temple and Helen.

But when we reached our bedroom, Miss Scatcherd was checking the drawers.

'Burns!' she said. 'Yours is far too untidy! Tomorrow, all day, you will wear a notice on your forehead saying UNTIDY!'

Helen said Miss Scatcherd was quite right, and wore the notice all the next day. But I was furious, and at the end of the afternoon, tore it off her head and threw it in the fire.

When Miss Temple received a letter from Dr Lloyd, agreeing that what I had said was true, she told the whole school that I had been wrongly accused and was not a liar. From that moment, I felt I was accepted, and set to work to learn as much as I could, and make as many friends as possible.

6

Learning to like school

Life at Lowood no longer seemed so hard, as spring approached. We enjoyed walking and playing in the surrounding countryside. But, with fog lying constantly in the valley, it was not a healthy place for a school, and by May more than half the girls were seriously ill with typhus fever. As a result of poor food and bad living conditions, many girls died.

While there was fear and death inside the school, the sun shone on the flowers outside, and on the flowing streams in the valleys. So I and the few who had escaped illness enjoyed the beautiful summer weather, with no lessons or discipline at all.

Helen Burns could not come walking with me, because she was ill, not with typhus but with tuberculosis. At first I had thought she would recover, but when I learned her illness was serious, I decided to visit her at night, for what might be the last time. I found her lying in bed, looking pale and weak.

'You've come to say goodbye,' she whispered, coughing. 'You are just in time. I'm going soon.'

'Where, Helen? Are you going home?' I asked.

'Yes, to my long home – my last home.'

'No, no, Helen!' I was crying at the thought of losing her.

'Jane, your feet are cold. Lie down with me and cover them with my blanket.' I did so.

'I am happy, Jane,' she continued. 'You mustn't cry. By dying young, I'll avoid suffering. I am going to heaven.'

'Does heaven really exist?' I asked.

'Yes, I'm sure of it. I'm sure our souls go there when we die,' she answered firmly.

'Will I see you again, Helen, when I die?'

'Yes, you will go to heaven too, Jane.'

I could not quite believe that heaven existed, and I held tightly to Helen. I did not want to let her go. We kissed goodnight and fell asleep. In the morning Miss Temple found me asleep, with Helen Burns dead in my arms. She was buried in the local churchyard.

Gradually the typhus fever left Lowood, but the number of deaths made the public aware of the poor conditions in which the pupils lived. Money was raised to build a new school in a better position, many improvements were made, and Mr Brocklehurst lost his position as manager. So it became a really useful place of education. I stayed for eight more years, for the last two as a teacher. I was busy and happy all that time, relying greatly on the help and encouragement of my dear friend Miss Temple.

But when she married and moved to a distant part of the country, I decided it was the moment for me to change my life too. I realized I had never known any other world apart from Lowood or Gateshead. Suddenly I wanted freedom . . . or at least a new master to serve. So I advertised in a newspaper for a job as a governess. When I received an answer from a Mrs Fairfax, who wanted a governess for a girl under ten years old, I accepted, with the permission of the new headmistress of Lowood.

7

Thornfield and Mr Rochester

Thornfield Hall was a large gentleman's house in the country, near a town called Millcote. There, after my sixteen-hour journey, I was welcomed by Mrs Fairfax. She was a little old lady, dressed in black, who seemed glad to have someone else to talk to, apart from the servants. Although the house was dark and frightening, with its big rooms full of heavy furniture, I was excited at being in a new place, and looked forward to my new life there, working for kind Mrs Fairfax.

But I was surprised to discover on my first full day at Thornfield that Mrs Fairfax was not in fact the owner, as I had assumed, but the housekeeper, and that my new master was a Mr Rochester, who was often away from home. My pupil was a girl called Adèle, seven or eight years old, who was born in France and could hardly speak English. Luckily I had learnt French very well at Lowood, and had no difficulty in communicating with young Adèle, a pretty, cheerful child. It appeared that Mr Rochester, who had known Adèle and her mother very well, had brought Adèle back to England to live with him after her mother had died. I taught her for several hours every day in the library, although it was not easy to make her concentrate on anything for long, as she was clearly not used to the discipline of lessons.

One day I took the opportunity of asking Mrs Fairfax a few questions about Mr Rochester, as I was curious about him, and the little housekeeper seemed happy to talk.

'Is he liked by most people?' was my first question.

'Oh yes, his family have always been respected here. They've owned the land round here for years,' she replied.

'But do *you* like him? What is his character like?'

'*I* have always liked him, and I think he's a fair master to his servants. He's a little peculiar, perhaps. He's travelled a lot, you know. I expect he's clever, but I can't tell, really.'

'What do you mean, *peculiar*?' I asked, interested.

'It's not easy to describe. You're never sure whether he's serious or joking. You don't really understand him, at least *I* don't. But that doesn't matter, he's a very good master.'

I could get no further information from Mrs Fairfax about Mr Rochester, but instead she offered to show me round the whole house. We went through many large, impressive rooms, finally reaching the top floor, where there was a narrow corridor with several small black doors, all shut. I stopped to look at them, and thought for a moment they looked like prison doors, hiding evil secrets. No sooner had I turned away to go downstairs than I heard a strange, ghostly laugh.

'Mrs Fairfax!' I called out, as the housekeeper was already on her way downstairs. 'Did you hear that laugh? Who is it?'

'It may be Grace Poole,' she answered calmly. 'She is paid to help the housemaid in her work, and always sews in one of those rooms.' I heard the laugh again. It did not sound human to me.

'Grace!' called Mrs Fairfax. I did not expect anyone to answer, but in fact a door opened and a middle-aged woman appeared. She looked too plain and sensible to be a ghost.

'Too much noise, Grace,' said Mrs Fairfax. 'Remember your instructions!' Grace nodded and went back into the room.

Several times in the next few months I went up to the top floor again, where I could look out of the high windows in the roof to see the surrounding countryside and be alone with my thoughts. I was very happy teaching pretty little Adèle in the daytime, and talking to kind old Mrs Fairfax in the evening, but I felt that something was missing from my life. I had dreams of a greater and better life, and above all, I wanted to *do* more. People are not always satisfied with a quiet life, and women as well as men need action.

While on the top floor I often heard Grace Poole's strange laugh, and sometimes I saw her too. She used to go silently in and out of the room with a plate of food or a glass of beer.

One day in January I had a free afternoon, as Adèle was ill, so I decided to walk to Hay, a village two miles away, to post a letter for the housekeeper. It was a bright, frosty day, and I was enjoying the fresh air and the exercise. Stopping on the lonely road, I watched the sun go down in the trees behind Thornfield, and then in the silence I heard a horse approaching. Suddenly there was a crash as the horse slipped and fell on the ice, bringing down its rider. I ran to see if I could help the traveller, who was swearing furiously as he pulled himself free of his horse.

'Are you hurt, sir? Can I do anything?' I asked.

'Just stand back,' he growled, as he lifted himself painfully to his feet. Obviously his leg hurt him, and he sat down quickly.

'If you need help, sir, I can fetch someone either from Thornfield Hall or from Hay,' I offered.

'Thank you, but I don't need anyone. I haven't broken any bones,' he replied crossly. I could see him clearly in the moonlight. He was of medium height, with wide shoulders and a strong chest. He had a dark face, with angry-looking eyes, and was about thirty-five. If he had been a young, attractive gentleman, I would have been too shy to offer help, but as he was not handsome, and even quite rough, I felt I wanted to help him.

'I can't leave you, sir, so late on this lonely road, till I see you are fit enough to get on your horse,' I insisted.

He looked at me for the first time when I said this.

'I think you ought to be at home yourself,' he answered. 'Do you live near here?'

'In that house over there,' I said, 'and I'm not at all afraid of being out at night. I'm just going to Hay to post a letter, and I'll be happy to take a message for you.'

'You live in . . . in that house?' he asked, surprised, pointing to Thornfield Hall, which was lit up in the moonlight.

'Yes, sir,' I replied.

'Whose house is it?' he asked.

'Mr Rochester's.'

'Do you know Mr Rochester?' was his next question.

'No, I've never seen him,' I answered.

'You aren't a servant at Thornfield Hall, of course. You must be . . .' he hesitated, looking at my plain black dress. He seemed puzzled to know who I was, so I helped him.

'I am the governess.'

'Ah, the governess! I had forgotten!' He tried to get up but his leg was still hurting him badly. 'I don't want you to fetch help, but you could help me yourself, if you like.'

'Of course, sir,' I said. And so he leaned his weight on my shoulder and I helped him walk to his horse. In a moment he had jumped on to the horse's back.

'Thank you, now take your letter to Hay, then hurry home!' he called as he rode off into the distance.

I walked on, glad to have helped someone, to have done something active for once. In my mind I saw that dark, strong face, and I still felt excited by our meeting. Even when I arrived back at Thornfield, I did not go in for a while. I did not want to go into the dark house, where I would spend the evening quietly with old Mrs Fairfax. So I stayed outside, staring up at the moon and the stars with a beating heart, wishing and dreaming of a different, more exciting life.

When I entered, the servants told me that Mr Rochester had arrived, and that he had hurt his leg when his horse slipped on ice on the road to Hay.

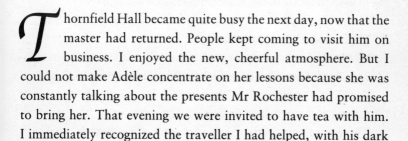 Getting to know Mr Rochester

T hornfield Hall became quite busy the next day, now that the master had returned. People kept coming to visit him on business. I enjoyed the new, cheerful atmosphere. But I could not make Adèle concentrate on her lessons because she was constantly talking about the presents Mr Rochester had promised to bring her. That evening we were invited to have tea with him. I immediately recognized the traveller I had helped, with his dark hair and skin, his square forehead and his stern look. His leg was supported on a chair, but he made no effort to greet me when I entered. In fact, he neither spoke nor moved.

'Have you brought a present for Miss Eyre with you as well?' Adèle asked him.

'A present? Who wants a present?' he said angrily. 'Did you expect a present, Miss Eyre? Do you like presents?'

'I haven't much experience of them, sir,' I answered. 'Anyway, I have no right to expect a present, as I haven't done anything to deserve one.'

'Don't be so modest! I've been talking to Adèle. She's not very clever, but you've taught her well.'

'Sir, that is my present. That's what a teacher wants most, praise of her pupil's progress.'

Mr Rochester drank his tea in silence. After tea, he called me closer to the fire, while Adèle played with Mrs Fairfax.

'Where were you before you came here?' he asked.

'I was at Lowood school, sir, for eight years.'

'Ah, yes, a charity school! Eight years! I'm surprised you lasted so long in such a place. There is something like magic in your face.

When I met you on the road to Hay last night, I almost thought you had put a spell on my horse! I still wonder if you did. What about your parents?'

'They're dead. I don't remember them.'

'And your relations?'

'I have none.'

'Who recommended you to come here?'

'I advertised, and Mrs Fairfax answered the advertisement.'

'Yes,' said the old housekeeper, 'and I thank God she did. She's a good teacher for Adèle, and a kind friend to me.'

'Don't try to give her a good character, Mrs Fairfax,' said Mr Rochester sternly. 'She and her magic made my horse slip on the ice last night.'

Mrs Fairfax looked puzzled and clearly did not understand.

'Miss Eyre,' continued Mr Rochester, 'how old were you when you started at Lowood?'

'About ten.'

'And you stayed there eight years, so you are now eighteen?' I nodded. 'I would never have been able to guess your age,' he went on. 'Now, what did you learn there? Can you play the piano?'

'A little.'

'Of course, that's what all young women say. Go and play a tune on the piano in the library.' I did as he asked.

'That's enough!' he called after a few minutes. 'Yes, you do indeed play a little, just like any schoolgirl, better than some perhaps. Now, bring me your sketches.' I fetched them from my room. Having looked carefully at them, he chose three.

'These are interesting,' he said. 'You have only expressed the shadow of your ideas, because you aren't good enough at drawing or painting, but the ideas, where did they come from? Who taught you to draw wind, and space, and feeling? But put them away now, Miss Eyre. Do you realize it's nine o'clock? Adèle should be in bed by now. Good night to you all.' Mr Rochester's mood had suddenly changed, and he clearly wished to be alone.

Later that evening I talked to Mrs Fairfax.

'You said Mr Rochester was *a little* peculiar,' I said.

'Well, what do you think, Miss Eyre?'

'I think he is *very* peculiar, and quite rude.'

'He may seem like that to a stranger. I'm so used to him that I never notice it. And he has had family troubles, you know.'

'But he has no family,' I answered.

'Not now, that's true, but he did have an older brother, who died nine years ago.'

'Nine years is a long time. Surely he has recovered from losing his brother by now.'

'Well, there was a lot of bad feeling in the family. The father was very fond of money, and wanted to keep the family property together, so the elder brother inherited most of it. I don't know what happened, but I do know Mr Edward (that's the master) quarrelled with his family. That's why he's travelled so much. When his brother died, he inherited Thornfield, but I'm not surprised he doesn't come here often.'

'Why should he stay away?' I asked, surprised.

'Perhaps he thinks it's a sad place. I really don't know.' It was clear that Mrs Fairfax would not tell me any more.

One evening, a few days later, I was invited to talk to Mr Rochester after dinner. At the far end of the room Adèle was delightedly telling Mrs Fairfax about the presents she had received. Mr Rochester called me closer to the fire.

'I don't like the conversation of children or old ladies,' he murmured to me. 'But they are entertaining each other at the moment, so I can amuse myself.' Tonight he did not look so stern, and there was a softness in his fine, dark eyes. As I was looking at him, he suddenly turned and caught my look.

'Do you think I'm handsome, Miss Eyre?' he asked.

Normally I would have taken time to think, and said something polite, but somehow I answered at once, 'No, sir.'

'Ah, you really are unusual! You are a quiet, serious little person, but you can be almost rude.'

'Sir, I'm sorry. I should have said that beauty doesn't matter, or something like that.'

'No, you shouldn't! I see, you criticize my appearance, and then you stab me in the back! All right, tell me. What is wrong with my appearance?'

'Mr Rochester, I didn't intend to criticize you.'

'Well, now you can. Look at my head. Do you think I am intelligent?' He pointed to his huge, square forehead.

'I do, sir. Is it rude to ask if you are also good?'

'Stabbing me again! Just because I said I didn't like talking to old ladies and children! Well, young lady, I wanted to be good when

'Sir, I'm sorry. I should have said that beauty doesn't matter, or something like that.'

I was younger, but life has been a struggle for me, and I've become as hard and tough as a rubber ball. I only have a little goodness left inside.' He was speaking rather excitedly, and I thought perhaps he had been drinking. 'Miss Eyre, you look puzzled. Tonight I want conversation. It's your turn. Speak.'

I said nothing, but smiled coldly.

'I'm sorry if I'm rude, Miss Eyre. But I'm twenty years older, and more experienced, than you. Don't you think I have the right to command you?'

'No, sir, not just because you're older and more experienced than me. You would have the right only if you'd made good use of your experience of life.'

'I don't accept that, as I've made very bad use of my experience! But will you agree to obey my orders anyway?'

I thought, 'He *is* peculiar, he's forgotten that he's paying me £30 a year to obey his orders,' and I said, 'Not many masters bother to ask if their servants are offended by their orders.'

'Of course! I'd forgotten that I pay you a salary! So will you agree because of the salary?'

'No, sir, not because of that, but because you forgot about it, and because you care whether a servant of yours is comfortable or not, I gladly agree.'

'You have honesty and feeling. There are not many girls like you. But perhaps I go too fast. Perhaps you have awful faults to counterbalance your few good points.'

'And perhaps you have too,' I thought.

He seemed to read my mind, and said quickly, 'Yes, you're right. I have plenty of faults. I went the wrong way when I was twenty-one, and have never found the right path again. I might have been very different. I might have been as good as you, and perhaps wiser. I am not a bad man, take my word for it, but I have done wrong. It wasn't my character, but circumstances which were to blame.

Why do I tell you all this? Because you're the sort of person people tell their problems and secrets to, because you're sympathetic and give them hope.'

'Do you think so, sir?'

'I do. You see, when life was difficult, I became desperate, and now all I have is regret.'

'Asking forgiveness might cure it, sir.'

'No, it won't. What I really should do is change my character, and I still could but – it's difficult. And if I can't have happiness, I want pleasure, even if it's wrong.'

'Pleasure may taste bitter, sir.'

'How do you know, a pure young thing like you? You have no experience of life and its problems. But I *will* try to lead a better life.'

I stood up. The conversation was becoming hard to follow.

'I must put Adèle to bed now,' I said.

'Don't be afraid of me, Miss Eyre. You don't relax or laugh very much, perhaps because of the effect Lowood school has had on you. But in time you will be more natural with me, and laugh, and speak freely. You're like a restless bird in a cage. When you get out of the cage, you'll fly very high. Good night.'

9

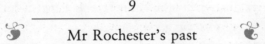

Mr Rochester's past

Soon I discovered what Mr Rochester meant when he said he had done wrong. One afternoon, while walking in the gardens of Thornfield, he told me the story of his love-affair in Paris with a French dancer, Céline.

'Yes, Miss Eyre, I was young and foolish then. I was so in love with her that I rented a house and hired servants for her. I gave her a carriage and jewels, in fact I threw away a fortune on her, just like any fool in love. One evening I visited her but found she was out, so I waited on her balcony, smoking a cigar. I heard her carriage arriving. Imagine my horror at seeing her step out followed by a man! You're so young, you've never felt love or jealousy, have you, Miss Eyre? You are floating along a quiet river now, you don't see the water boiling at the foot of the great rocks, but one day you'll come to a point in life's stream where the wild force of the waves may destroy you, where the noisy rushing water may drown you! I am calm enough now, calm enough to like living here at Thornfield. I like it because it's old, and grey, and dark, and yet I hate — ' He did not finish what he was saying, staring angrily up at the windows on the top floor of his house. It was a look of disgust, pain and shame. I could not understand what he meant, and wanted to hear more about Céline, so I encouraged him to finish the story.

'What happened when she entered the house, sir?'

'Oh, I'd forgotten Céline! By the way, it's strange my telling you all this, but I know my secret's safe with you, and I know, too, that it can't have an evil influence on you – your mind's too strong for that. Yes, I listened to her conversation with her lover, an elegant young fool, and I knew I was no longer in love with her. So I walked into the room, told her our relationship was over, and challenged her lover to fight me. Next day I shot him in the arm during our fight, thought that was the end of the whole thing, and left France. But a few months before, Céline had had a baby girl, Adèle, and she claimed that Adèle was my child. She may be, although I doubt it. So when, a few years later, Céline abandoned Adèle and ran away to Italy with a singer, I went to Paris and brought Adèle back to grow up in England.'

I felt proud that Mr Rochester had trusted me with the story of his past life. I thought a lot about his character, and although I was aware of his faults, I also saw his goodness and kindness to me.

From now on, my happiest moments were spent with him. I could not have imagined a better companion.

One night I was woken by a slight noise. I felt sure someone was outside my bedroom door. As I hurried to lock it, I called, 'Who's there?' There was a strange, inhuman sound, then I heard a door shut upstairs on the top floor. 'Was that Grace Poole?' I wondered, trembling. My curiosity made me open the door, and I found the corridor full of smoke. I saw it was coming from Mr Rochester's door, which was slightly open. I completely forgot my fears and rushed into his room. He lay fast asleep, surrounded by flames and smoke. Even his sheets were on fire.

'Wake up! Wake up!' I shouted desperately, throwing water over him to put out the flames. Not until the fire was almost out did he wake up, swearing to find himself so wet.

Mr Rochester lay fast asleep, surrounded by flames and smoke.

'Is there a flood?' he cried.

'No, sir,' I answered, 'but there's been a fire.'

'Jane Eyre, is it you and your magic?' he asked. 'Have you put a spell on me again? Did you intend to drown me this time?'

'Please get up, sir. Someone has plotted to kill you!' and I explained what I had heard and how I had put out the fire. He looked very serious, and thought for a few seconds.

'Shall I fetch Mrs Fairfax, sir, or the servants?' I asked.

'No, why bother them? Just stay here for a moment. I'm going up to the top floor. Don't call anyone. I'll be back soon.'

I waited, cold and tired, in his room for what seemed a very long time. Then I saw the light of his candle approaching through the darkness, and he appeared, looking pale and depressed.

'Did you see anything when you opened your bedroom door?' he asked, glancing sharply at me.

'No, sir, only a candle on the floor.'

'But you heard a strange laugh, did you say?'

'Yes, I've heard it before. Grace Poole laughs like that.'

'That's it. It must have been Grace Poole. You've guessed it. I shall consider what to do about it. But meanwhile I'm glad you're the only person who knows anything about all this. Say nothing to anybody else, and now, go back to your own room.'

'Good night, then, sir,' I said, moving towards the door.

'What! Are you leaving me already!' he said, seeming surprised, although he had just told me to go, 'and so coldly?'

'You said I should go, sir.'

'But not without saying goodbye, not without a kind word or two. Why, you've saved my life. I hate being in debt to anyone, but with you it's different, Jane. I'm happy to owe you my life.' His voice was trembling as he took both my hands in his. 'I knew, when I first saw you, that you would do me good. I saw it in your eyes when I met you. I was right to . . . like . . . your smile and the magic

in your face.' There was energy in his voice and a strange light in
his eyes.

'I'm glad I happened to be awake,' I said, 'but I must go now.
I'm cold.' I knew I could not control my feelings much longer, and
I needed time to think. But he still held on to my hands. Then I
thought of a way of escaping.

'I think I hear the servants moving, sir,' I said.

'Well, leave me,' he said, and let me go.

That night, or what was left of it, I could not sleep. My mind
was full of confusing pictures and disturbed emotions.

10

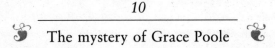

The mystery of Grace Poole

After this sleepless night I was eager to see Mr Rochester in
the morning, but there was no sign of him. He had obviously
told the servants that he had accidentally set fire to his room
by knocking over a lighted candle. As I passed his bedroom, I saw
Grace Poole sitting inside, calmly mending the curtains. She
certainly did not look desperate or mad enough to have tried to
murder her master. But I decided to investigate.

'Good morning, Grace,' I said, entering the room. 'Tell me, what
happened last night? The servants are talking about it.'

'Good morning, miss,' she replied, looking up innocently. 'Well,
master was reading in bed and fell asleep, so he must have knocked
the candle over. It set fire to the sheets, but luckily he managed to
put the flames out with some water.'

'How strange!' I said quietly. 'Didn't anybody hear what was
happening?' At this, she seemed to examine me carefully.

'Mrs Fairfax and you sleep nearest this room, miss. Mrs Fairfax is a heavy sleeper, like most old people, and didn't hear anything. But you're young, miss. Perhaps you heard a noise?'

'I did,' I whispered. 'I'm sure I heard a strange laugh.'

She went on sewing calmly.

'I don't think master would have laughed, when he was in such danger,' she said. 'You must have been dreaming.'

'No, I wasn't dreaming,' I replied sharply.

'You didn't think of opening your door and looking out into the corridor?' she asked. I suddenly realized that if she suspected I knew of her guilt, she might attack *me*.

'No, in fact I locked my door,' I answered, 'and I shall lock it every night from now on.'

'That's wise of you, miss. We might have burglars at Thornfield one day, you never know.'

I was amazed by her self-control, and could not understand why Mr Rochester had not asked the police to arrest her, or at least dismissed her from his service. Why had he asked me to keep the attack a secret? How could such a proud gentleman be so much in the power of one of his servants that he could not even punish her for trying to kill him? Did she know a terrible secret from his past, which she had threatened to tell? Could he ever have been in love with her? 'No,' I thought, 'he could never love anyone as plain and coarse as she is. But then, I'm not beautiful either, and I sometimes think he loves me. Last night – his words, his look, his voice!' And my cheeks were red as I thought of those precious moments.

I was now even more impatient to see Mr Rochester, but when I was having tea with Mrs Fairfax in the afternoon, the first thing she said was, 'It's fine weather for the master's journey.'

'Journey!' I cried. 'I didn't know he'd gone anywhere!'

'Oh yes, he went off just after breakfast, to visit a family in a big house about sixteen miles away. I know they've invited a lot of guests, who'll be staying in the house. Mr Rochester is always very popular with the ladies at these parties, so he may not come back for a week or so.'

'Who are the ladies at this house-party?'

'Three sisters, very elegant young ladies, and their friends, Blanche and Mary Ingram. But Blanche is the most beautiful of all. I saw her when she came to a Christmas party at Thornfield, six or seven years ago.'

'What does she look like?'

'She was eighteen then, a lovely girl, with beautiful skin, long curling black hair, and fine black eyes which shone as brightly as her jewels. She looked like a queen. All the gentlemen admired her, not only for her beauty but also for her musical skills. When she and Mr Rochester sang together, it was a delight to hear.'

'Mr Rochester? I didn't know he could sing.'

'Oh yes, he has a very fine voice. And then she played the piano later. The master said she played extremely well.'

'And this beautiful lady isn't married yet?'

'No, I don't think she or her sister has much money.'

'But I'm surprised some rich gentleman hasn't fallen in love with her. Mr Rochester, for example. He's rich, isn't he?'

'Oh yes. But you see, there's a considerable difference in age. He's nearly forty, and she's only twenty-five.'

'Well, marriages like that happen every day. Do you think —' But I was interrupted by Adèle, who came to join us, and the subject was changed.

That night in my room I was stern with myself.

'You, Jane Eyre,' I accused my reflection in the mirror, 'you are the biggest fool in the world! How could you imagine that a gentleman of family and wealth would love *you*, a plain little governess! Just look at yourself!' And I decided that next day I would draw an honest sketch of myself, and then one of Blanche Ingram, painting the most lovely face I could imagine, according to

Mrs Fairfax's description. In the future, if ever my old feelings about Mr Rochester began to return, I would only have to glance at the two pictures to see the great difference between us, and in this way common sense would destroy my foolish dreams.

11

The Thornfield house-party

*T*wo disappointing weeks passed before we heard from Mr Rochester again. During this time I tried hard to forget my feeling for him. I reminded myself that he paid me to teach Adèle, nothing more, and that no other relationship could exist between us. When his letter finally came, Mrs Fairfax announced with great excitement that he was planning a house-party at Thornfield. He was going to return in three days' time, and had invited a large number of ladies and gentlemen to stay for several days. We all worked extremely hard in the next few days, cleaning all the rooms and preparing the food.

The only person in the house who did not appear excited was Grace Poole, who stayed in her room upstairs, coming down once a day for food and drink. None of the servants seemed at all curious about her, but I once heard two of the maids talking, and I listened when I caught her name.

'Does Grace Poole earn a lot, then?' asked one.

'Oh yes, five times what you and I earn!' answered the other.

'But she's good at the work, I expect,' said the first.

'Ah! She understands what she has to do, that's true,' answered the second, 'and not everyone would want to do her job, not even for all that money!'

'Quite right! I wonder whether the master —' Suddenly they saw me and broke off their conversation.

'Doesn't she know?' I heard one of them whisper.

'No,' said the other, and they were silent. So I realized there was a secret at Thornfield, which nobody wanted to tell me.

At last the great day came. Everything was ready for the master and his guests. Adèle and I watched from an upstairs window as the carriages arrived. In front rode Mr Rochester on his black horse, and with him rode a beautiful lady, her black curls streaming in the wind. 'Blanche Ingram!' I thought. We listened to the laughing and talking in the hall, as the guests were welcomed by their host and his housekeeper. From a dark corner of the stairs we admired the ladies as they went up to their rooms, and then again as they descended to dinner in their elegant evening dresses. Adèle was hoping Mr Rochester would call her down to meet the guests, but in the end she was so tired with all the excitement that she and I both went to bed early.

Next morning after breakfast the whole group went out for the day. Again I saw Mr Rochester and Blanche Ingram riding together. I pointed this out to Mrs Fairfax.

'You see, Mr Rochester clearly prefers her to any of the other ladies.'

'Yes, he does seem to admire her,' admitted the housekeeper.

'And *she* admires *him*. Notice how she looks at him! But I haven't really seen her face yet. I'd like to.'

'You'll see her tonight,' answered Mrs Fairfax. 'I mentioned to the master that Adèle wanted to be introduced to the ladies, and he asked you to bring her down to meet them this evening.'

'Well, I'll go if he wants me to, but I don't like meeting strangers. I'm not used to it.'

'I understand how you feel,' said the old lady kindly, 'but the guests won't notice you much, and you can easily escape after a short time.'

So Adèle and I, dressed in our best, were waiting as the ladies came into the sitting-room after dinner. I was most impressed by the beauty and elegance of all of them, but was especially fascinated by the Ingram family. Lady Ingram, although between forty and fifty, was still a fine woman. Her hair still looked black, by candle-light at least, and her teeth still seemed perfect. But she had fierce, proud eyes, that reminded me of aunt Reed's, and a hard, powerful voice. Her daughter Mary was rather quiet, but her other daughter Blanche was very different. As soon as the gentlemen came into the room and coffee was served, she became the centre of attention. She played the piano excellently, she sang sweetly, she discussed intelligently, and all the time her flashing eyes, rich black curls and fine figure attracted glances from every gentleman in the room.

But I was looking for someone else. The last time I had seen him, on the night of the fire, he had held my hands, told me I had saved his life, and looked at me as if he loved me. How close we had been then! But now, he entered the room without even looking at me, and took a seat with the ladies. I could not stop looking at him, rather like a thirsty man who knows the water is poisoned but cannot resist drinking. I had never intended to love him. I had tried hard to destroy all feelings of love for him, but now that I saw him again, I could not stop myself loving him. I compared him to the other gentlemen present. They were all fine, handsome men, but they did not have his power, his character, his strength, or indeed his deep laugh or his gentle smile. I felt that he and I were the same sort of person, that there was something in my brain and heart, in my blood and bone, that connected me to him for ever. And although I knew I must hide my feelings, must never allow myself to hope, I also knew that while there was breath in my body, I would always love him.

Just then I heard Blanche Ingram say to him,

'Mr Rochester, you should have sent that little girl – Adèle, is that her name? – to school, but I see you have a governess for her.

I saw a strange little person with her just now. Has she gone? Oh no, there she is on the window-seat. It's very foolish of you, you know. Governesses aren't worth their salary, are they, Mamma?'

'My dear, don't mention governesses to me!' cried Lady Ingram, holding a white hand to her forehead. 'How I have suffered with them!' One of the older ladies whispered to her, pointing in my direction.

'Oh, I don't care if she hears me!' said Lady Ingram. 'All governesses are useless. They never teach children anything.'

'What fun we used to have, playing tricks on them, didn't we, Mary?' laughed Blanche. 'But governesses are boring. Let's change the subject. Mr Rochester, will you sing with me?'

'With pleasure,' he answered, bowing, and the group moved towards the piano. This was the moment for me to escape, but I had only just left the sitting-room and reached the hall, when Mr Rochester appeared through another door.

'Come back, you're leaving too early,' he said to me.

'I'm tired, sir.' He looked at me for a minute.

'And a little depressed. Why? Tell me.'

'Nothing – it's nothing, sir. I'm not depressed.'

'But I think you are. You're almost crying. But I haven't got time now to discover the reason. Well, tonight you may leave early, but I want to see you with my guests every evening. Good night, my—' He stopped, bit his lip, and turned quickly away.

Those were cheerful, busy days at Thornfield. The old house had never seen so much life and activity. When it was fine the host and his guests went riding, visited places of interest, and walked in the gardens, and when it was wet they played games indoors. Mr Rochester and Blanche Ingram were always together. Observing them closely, I felt very sure that he would soon marry this fine lady. But I did not feel jealous, because *I knew he did not love her*. She had made every effort to attract him, but he had not given her his heart. I saw her faults very clearly. She was intelligent but had no opinions of her own. She was beautiful but not good. She spoke of feelings but she knew nothing of sympathy or pity. And above all she had her mother's pride and hardness. Other eyes apart from mine saw all these faults. Mr Rochester himself knew she was not perfect, but he was clearly preparing to marry her, perhaps because she was of good family, perhaps for some other reason.

One day when Mr Rochester was out alone on business, a stranger arrived in a carriage, and introduced himself as an old friend of the master's. His name was Mason, and he had just returned from the West Indies, where Mr Rochester had once lived.

12

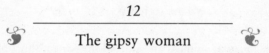

The gipsy woman

No sooner had Mr Mason joined the group of guests than a servant entered to announce the arrival of an old gipsy woman, who was supposed to be a skilled fortune-teller. The ladies were very excited and decided to ask her to tell their fortunes. Miss Ingram, as usual, was first, and spent fifteen minutes alone with the old woman in the library. She came back looking cross.

'It's just childish nonsense! How can you all believe in that sort of thing!' she said, picking up a book and pretending to read it. But as she frowned more and more, and did not turn a page, I assumed that the gipsy's words were more important to her than she wanted us to think. Next, three young ladies went in together, and came back full of praise for the gipsy's skill.

'She's old, and dirty, and ugly!' they cried, shocked, 'but she knows everything about us, everything!' While the gentlemen were calming them down, the servant entered the room again.

'Excuse me, miss,' he said to me. 'The gipsy says there's another young single lady in the room. She refuses to leave the house until she has seen all the young ladies. It must be you.'

'Oh, I'll go,' I said gladly. I was curious to see the gipsy.

She was sitting in an armchair in the library, murmuring words over a little black book. Her large black hat covered most of her face, but when she lifted her head, I saw her dark eyes.

'So you want me to tell your fortune?' she asked.

'Well, I must warn you, I don't believe in your skill.'

'I expected that. Why don't you tremble?'

'I'm not cold.'

'Why don't you turn pale?'

'I'm not ill.'

'Why don't you ask me to tell your fortune?'

'I'm not a fool.'

The old woman laughed and started smoking a short black pipe.

'I can prove that you're cold, *and* ill, *and* a fool,' she said. 'Listen. You're cold, because you're alone. You're ill, because you lack love. And you're a fool, because love is near you, and you won't take one step to reach it.'

'That's true of many people,' I said, interested.

'Yes, but especially true of you. I can see that happiness is waiting for you, if you really want it. Tell me, in that room of fine people, isn't there one face you look at, one person you're interested in?'

'I hardly know the ladies and gentlemen here,' I answered.

'Well, you surely know the master of the house? What do you think of his relationship with his guests, and with one particular guest?' asked the gipsy, smiling wickedly.

'They're all very friendly with each other,' I replied cautiously. The gipsy seemed to know a lot about Thornfield.

'Friendly! I'd say more than that, in fact I'd go so far as to mention the name of Blanche Ingram and the word, marriage. They will obviously be an extremely happy couple, although I told Miss Ingram something about the Rochester property which made her look quite depressed. If a wealthier gentleman comes along, Mr Rochester might lose his beautiful bride . . .'

'But I came to hear about *my* future, not Mr Rochester's!'

'It depends on whether you're going to stretch out your hand for happiness. Let me look at your face. Your eyes and your mouth show me that feelings are important to you, but your forehead shows me that common sense is your main guide in life. You will never do anything wrong or shameful. Well, I respect that. I don't want sacrifice or sorrow in my life. I want – but that will do. I'd like to stay here looking at you for ever, but I must stop acting now.'

Was I dreaming? What was happening? The old woman's voice had changed and become as familiar to me as my own.

'Well, Jane, do you know me?' asked the familiar voice. And, struggling with the old clothes, Mr Rochester stepped out of his disguise.

'Sir, you've been talking nonsense to make *me* talk nonsense. It's hardly fair.'

'Do you forgive me, Jane?'

'I shall try to, sir. But you shouldn't have done it.'

'What are my guests doing, Jane?'

'Discussing the gipsy, I imagine. Oh, and did you know that a stranger has arrived to see you?'

'A stranger! I wasn't expecting anyone. Who can it be?'

'His name's Mason, sir, and he comes from the West Indies.'

The smile froze on Mr Rochester's lips, and his face went white.

'Mason! The West Indies!' he repeated three times.

'Do you feel ill, sir?' I asked, worried.

'Jane, help me,' he murmured, almost falling. I helped him to sit down, and sat with him. He took my hand and rubbed it gently.

'I wish I were on an island with you and nobody else, with no trouble or danger or terrible memories to make me suffer.'

'How can I help you, sir? I'd give my life to help you.'

'Jane, if I need help, I'll ask you, I promise. Get me a glass of wine now.' I fetched one from the dining-room, and gave it to him. He looked less pale, but very stern.

'Jane, if all those fine guests of mine came and spat at me, what would you do?' he asked.

'Turn them out of the house, sir, if I could.'

'But if they only looked at me coldly, and whispered behind their hands about me, and then left me one by one?'

'I'd stay with you, sir, to comfort you.'

'And if the whole world disapproved of me, would you still stay with me?'

'If you deserved my friendship, as I'm sure you do, I wouldn't care about other people's disapproval.'

'Thank you, Jane. Now go and ask Mr Mason to come and see me.' So I did, and, leaving the two men in the library, went to bed. Much later I heard him showing Mr Mason to his bedroom, and was glad that Mr Rochester sounded so cheerful.

13

The stranger is attacked

I was woken by the full moon shining in on me, as I had forgotten to draw my curtains. Suddenly, a wild, terrible cry broke the silence, echoing throughout the house. My heart missed a beat. What could it mean? It came from the top floor. Then I heard the sounds of a desperate struggle, just above my room.

'Help! Help! Help! Won't anyone help me? Rochester! Rochester! For God's sake, come!' shouted a voice from upstairs.

Bedroom doors were opened as the guests woke up. 'What's happening?' 'Fetch a candle!' 'Is it a fire?' 'Are there burglars?' 'Where's Rochester? He isn't in his room!'

'Here I am!' called the master of the house, descending with a candle from the top floor. 'It's all right. Don't be afraid, ladies. A servant's had a bad dream, that's all, and started screaming. Nothing to worry about. Please go back to your rooms. You'll catch cold otherwise.' And so he calmed his guests and persuaded them to return to their rooms.

But I knew that the sounds I had heard could have nothing to do with a servant's dream. So I dressed and waited in my room, in case I was needed. After about an hour, when Thornfield Hall was completely silent again, there was a cautious knock on my door.

'Are you awake, Jane?' asked the voice I had been expecting.

'Yes, sir, and dressed.'

'Good, I need you. Come and help me. Bring a clean cloth with you.' We went quietly up to the top floor, where he unlocked one of the small black doors.

'Do you feel faint at the sight of blood?' he asked.

'I don't think so,' I replied. We entered a room with curtains hung on the walls. One of the curtains was tied back to reveal a secret door into another small room. From there came an angry growling sound, almost like a dog.

'Wait here,' said Mr Rochester, and went into the secret room where a shout of laughter greeted him. Ah, so Grace Poole was there! He came out quickly and closed the secret door. Then he showed me why he needed me. In an armchair lay Mr Mason, his clothes and his arm covered in blood. As we bent over him, he opened his eyes and groaned.

'Am I going to die?' he murmured weakly.

'No, man, don't be foolish. It's just a scratch,' answered Mr Rochester. 'Now Jane,' turning to me, 'I'll have to leave you in this room with Mason while I fetch the doctor. You must wipe away the blood with the damp cloth, like this, and help him to drink a little water. But on no account must you speak to him. Is that understood?' I nodded, and nervously watched him leave the room. I could hear him turning the key in the lock.

So here I was, in the middle of the night, locked in with a bleeding, dying man, and a wild, murdering woman only the other side of a door! It seemed a long night, interrupted only by Mason's groans, and by occasional animal-like noises from the secret room. I had plenty of time to wonder why these violent attacks happened, first the fire in Mr Rochester's room, and now a physical attack on a stranger. And how was Mr Mason involved? Why was he here on the top floor? I had heard his host showing him to a bedroom near mine, on the second floor. And why was Mr Rochester so frightened when Mr Mason came to Thornfield?

At last Mr Rochester arrived with the doctor, who cleaned and bandaged Mason's wounds.

'Strange!' remarked the doctor. 'The skin on the shoulder has been torn by teeth, as well as a knife!'

'She bit me,' murmured Mason, 'when Rochester managed to get the knife from her.'

'Well, I warned you not to see her alone,' said Rochester. 'You should have waited till the morning, then we could have seen her together. Don't worry, man, when you get back to the West Indies, you can forget her. Think of her as dead and buried. Now, doctor, is Mason ready to be moved? I have a carriage waiting outside. You'll take him home with you to avoid gossip, and then in a few days he'll be fit enough to leave the country.'

Although it was now early morning, the house was still in total silence, and so there were no witnesses to see Mason being helped downstairs and put in the carriage.

'Look after him, doctor,' said Rochester. 'Goodbye, Dick.'

'Edward, make sure she's taken care of, make sure she's treated well . . .' Mason could not continue, but burst into tears.

'I'll do my best, Dick, as I always have done,' replied Rochester, shutting the door of the carriage, which rolled away. 'But I wish there was an end to it!' he murmured to himself.

As we were walking back through the garden to the house, he said to me, 'Jane, you've had a strange night. You look pale. Were you afraid when I left you alone with Mason?'

'Not of Mason, sir, but of Grace Poole in the secret room.'

'But I'd locked her door. I would never leave you in danger.'

'Will she go on living here, sir?' I asked.

'Oh yes. Don't think about her.'

'But I'm sure your life is in danger while she's here.'

'Don't worry, I can take care of myself. I'm in more danger while Mason's in England. I live in constant fear of a disaster.'

'But Mr Mason's weak! You have great influence with him!'

'Yes. He wouldn't knowingly hurt me, but by one careless word he could destroy, if not my life, at least my chance of happiness. Sit down with me on this bench, Jane. I want to ask you something.' The early sun warmed the bench and the birds were singing. 'Now, Jane, suppose a boy in a foreign country makes a mistake, not a *crime*, mind you. The results of this mistake have a terrible effect on his whole life. He comes home after years of suffering, and meets – someone, who is fresh and good and pure. Now, can he ignore society, can he forget the past, and live the rest of his life with her in peace?'

It was a difficult question to answer. In the end I said,

'You can't rely on a human being to cure you of evil and give you peace. You must ask God's help.'

'But I think I've found the cure! It's . . .' He paused. I held my breath. I almost thought the birds would stop singing to hear the name he was going to say.

'Yes,' he said in quite a different, hard voice, 'you've noticed my love for Miss Ingram, haven't you? Don't you think she'll cure me of my wickedness, Jane? Oh, I can hear some of the guests in the garden. Go into the house by the back door.' As I went one way, and he another, I heard him say cheerfully to the gentlemen, 'Mason's already left. I got up early to say goodbye to him.'

14

Trouble at Gateshead

When I was a child at Gateshead, Bessie the nursemaid used to say that to dream of children was a sure sign of trouble to come. For a whole week now I had dreamed of a small child every night, and perhaps Bessie was right, as a message came from Gateshead.

It appeared that my cousin John Reed, who had spent and wasted all his money and some of his mother's, and been in debt or in prison most of his life, had killed himself a week before. And then Mrs Reed, whose health had been badly affected by worrying about her son, had suddenly fallen ill when she heard of his death. Although she could hardly speak, she had recently managed to express a wish to see me. And so my cousins Eliza and Georgiana had sent their coachman, Robert, to bring me back to Gateshead.

I felt I could not refuse to see my aunt, perhaps for the last time. So I went to ask Mr Rochester's permission to leave Thornfield for a while. I found him talking to Miss Ingram, who looked at me in disgust when I interrupted their conversation.

'Well, Jane, what is it?' he asked, when we had left the room full of guests and gone into the library.

'Please, sir, I would like permission to visit my aunt, who is ill, for a week or two.'

'Your aunt! You told me you had no relations!'

'I have none who love me, sir. She's Mrs Reed, my uncle's wife. Her son has died recently. I really can't neglect her now that she is dying.'

'What nonsense, Jane, rushing off to visit an old lady who has never loved you! But I see you've decided to go. Where does she live and how long will you stay?'

'She lives at Gateshead, sir, a hundred miles away. I'll stay as short a time as I can.'

'Promise me only to stay a week.'

'I can't promise, sir, I might have to stay longer.'

'And you certainly can't travel a hundred miles alone!'

'They've sent the coachman for me, sir. I'll leave tomorrow.'

Mr Rochester thought for a while.

'Well, you'll need some money. I haven't paid you any salary yet. How much have you in the world, Jane?' he asked, smiling.

I showed him my tiny purse. He took it and laughed as he counted the few coins. Then he took out his wallet.

'Here is £50,' he said, offering me a note.

'But you only owe me £15, sir!' I cried.

'On second thoughts, give me that back. If you had £50, perhaps you would stay away for three months. Here is £10. Is that enough?'

'Now you owe me £5, sir,' I pointed out.

'You'll have to come back for it then,' he said, laughing.

'There's something else, sir. You've told me you're going to marry soon. In that case, Adèle should go to boarding school.'

'To get her out of my lovely bride's way? A very sensible suggestion. But what about you?'

'I must find another job somewhere. I'll advertise.'

'Don't you dare!' he growled. 'Promise me, Jane, not to look for another job. I'll take care of that.'

'I'll promise, sir, if you promise that Adèle and I will be out of your house before your bride enters it.'

'Very well! And now we must say goodbye.'

'Goodbye, Mr Rochester.'

I set out early the next morning and travelled all day. As I approached Gateshead Hall, I realized it was nine years since I had left it. In that time I had made some friends, gained much self-confidence, and finally lost my hatred of the Reeds.

I was delighted to see my old friend Bessie again. She had married Robert the coachman, and was very busy with her three young children. The house itself had not changed at all, but my cousins certainly had. Eliza was now very tall and thin, with a rather sour face, dressed in very plain clothes, and with a cross hanging round her neck. Georgiana, on the other hand, was still pretty but very fat, and wore extremely fashionable clothes. They did not seem pleased to see me, in fact they more or less ignored me, but I hardly noticed their rudeness. I told the housekeeper that I would be staying for several days, and then went straight to my aunt's room.

I remembered it well from my childhood. I had often been called there to be punished. Bending over her bed I kissed her.

'How are you, dear aunt?' I asked. I had sworn never to call her aunt again, but I did not regret breaking that promise to myself. I held her hand.

'Are you Jane Eyre?' she asked. Her face, although deathly pale, was as stern as ever, and she removed her hand from mine. 'That child was more trouble to me than anyone would believe! I was glad to send her to Lowood. And John! Poor John! He needs so much money! Where can I get more money from? What will happen?' She seemed very confused and excited, so I left her to sleep.

Her illness got worse in the next few days. I spent some time every day looking after her, and the rest of the time with my cousins, listening to their plans for the future. Eliza was planning to join a religious community after her mother's death, but Georgiana was hoping to stay in London with relations, to see the new fashions and go to all the parties. It was quite clear they had no real feeling for their mother, and were almost looking forward to her death.

One dark, stormy night I visited the dying woman. She lay there asleep in her room, neglected by her daughters and servants. As I looked out of the window into the black emptiness, I wondered about the great mystery of death, and thought of Helen Burns, who was so sure her spirit would go to heaven. Would my aunt's spirit go there too?

'Who are you?' I heard the sick woman murmuring. 'I wanted to see Jane Eyre. I must tell her something.'

'I *am* Jane Eyre, aunt,' I told her gently.

'I know I'm very ill,' she said weakly. 'Before I die I must confess what I've done wrong. First, I broke my promise to my husband about you, and second—' She broke off. 'After all, perhaps I don't need to tell her,' she said to herself. And then, 'No, it's no good, I know I'm dying. I must tell her, and quickly! Jane Eyre, take the letter from the top drawer of my desk, and read it.' I did so. It said:

Madeira

Dear Mrs Reed,

    Please inform me of the address of my niece, Jane Eyre. As I am unmarried, with no children, and fairly wealthy, I would like her to come to Madeira to live with me, and to inherit all my property when I die.

John Eyre

'Why did I never hear of this?' I asked, amazed.

'I hated you so much that I wrote back to him, telling him you had died of typhus fever at Lowood. That was my revenge on you, for causing me so much trouble!' she cried angrily.

'Dear aunt,' I said, 'don't think about that any more. I was only a child, it's not surprising I was a nuisance.'

'You were always so angry and violent, such a wicked child!'

'Not as wicked as you think. I would have loved you if you'd let me. Forget it all and kiss me now, aunt.' But it was too late for her to break the habit of dislike, and she turned away from me. Poor woman! She died soon afterwards, keeping her hatred of me alive in her heart, and no one at Gateshead cried for her.

15

The future Mrs Rochester

And so I set out on the long journey back to Thornfield. Mrs Fairfax had written to me while I was at Gateshead, telling me that the guests had all gone, and Mr Rochester had gone to London to buy a carriage for his wedding. It was clear that he would be getting married very soon.

After a long day sitting in the coach, I decided to get out at Millcote, leave my luggage at the hotel, and walk across the fields to Thornfield. It was a warm June evening, and I felt glad to be going home. I had to remind myself sternly that Thornfield was not my permanent home, and that the person I was so looking forward to seeing was perhaps not even thinking of me.

And then I saw him! He was sitting on the gate ahead of me, writing in a notebook. He noticed me at once.

'Hallo!' he cried. I was trembling at the unexpected sight of him, and could not control my voice, so I approached in silence.

'So it's Jane Eyre!' he continued. 'Why didn't you send for a carriage? It's just like you to come on foot from Millcote. Now, what have you been doing for a whole month?'

'I've been looking after my aunt, sir, who's just died.'

'You come from another world, Jane, from the world of the dead. I think you must be a spirit. And absent for a whole month! I'm sure you've quite forgotten me.'

Even though I knew I would soon lose him, he had such power to make me happy that I was in heaven listening to him.

'Did Mrs Fairfax tell you I've been to London?' he asked.

'Oh yes, sir, she did.'

'And I expect she told you why I went there? Well, you must see the carriage I've bought, Jane. It will suit Mrs Rochester perfectly. I only wish I were more handsome, as she's so beautiful. Can't you put one of your spells on me, to make me more attractive for her?'

'That's beyond the power of magic, sir,' I replied, while thinking 'To someone who loves you, you are handsome enough.'

Mr Rochester was sometimes able to read my thoughts, but this time he just smiled warmly at me, and opened the gate.

'Pass, friend,' he said, 'and welcome home!'

I could have just walked past him in silence, but something made me turn and say quickly, before I could stop myself, 'Thank you, Mr Rochester, for your great kindness. I'm glad to come back to you, and wherever you are is my home – my only home.' I ran across the field and into the house before he had time to answer.

Two weeks passed after my return, with no news of the wedding. There were no preparations at Thornfield, and no visits to the Ingram family, who lived only a few miles away. I almost began to hope.

It was the middle of summer, and every day the sun shone on the green fields, the white, baked roads, and the cool, dark woods. One evening, after Adèle had gone to sleep, I went into the garden. I discovered a quiet place where I thought nobody would find me, but then I noticed Mr Rochester had come into the garden too. Hoping to escape back to the house, I crept quietly behind him while he was bending over to admire an insect, but—

'Jane,' he said suddenly, 'come and look at this beautiful insect.

Oh, now he's flown away. No, don't go back to the house, Jane, on such a lovely night. Come and walk with me.' I could not find a reason for leaving him, so I accompanied him in silence.

'Jane,' he began, 'you like Thornfield, don't you? And you even like little Adèle, and old Mrs Fairfax, don't you?'

'I do, sir, I really don't want to leave them.'

'What a pity!' he sighed. 'That's what happens in life. No sooner have you got used to a place than you have to move on.'

'Do I have to move on, sir? Leave Thornfield?'

'I'm afraid you must, Jane.'

'Then you *are* going to be married, sir?'

'Exactly, Jane. And as you have pointed out, when I take the lovely Miss Ingram as my bride, you and Adèle must leave the house, so I'm looking for a new job for you.'

'I'm sorry to cause you trouble,' I said miserably.

'No trouble at all! In fact I've already heard of a very good job which would be just right for you, teaching the five daughters of an Irish family. You'll like Ireland, I think. They're such friendly people,' he said cheerfully.

'It's such a long way away, sir!' I was fighting to keep my tears back. There was an icy coldness in my heart.

'Away from what, Jane?'

'From England and from Thornfield and—'

'Well?'

'From *you*, sir!' I could not stop myself, and burst into tears immediately.

'It certainly is very far away,' he said calmly. 'Let's sit on this bench, Jane, like old friends saying goodbye. You know, I sometimes feel as if you and I were connected by a string tying our two hearts together, and if you went to Ireland, I think that string might break and I might bleed to death.'

'I wish . . . I wish I'd never been born!' I cried. 'I wish I'd never come to Thornfield!' No longer able to control my feelings, I poured out what was in my heart. 'I can't bear to leave! Because here I've been treated kindly. And because I've met you, Mr Rochester, and I can't bear never to see you again. Now I have to leave, I feel as if I'm dying!'

'Why do you have to leave?' he asked innocently.

'Why?' I repeated, amazed. 'Because you're marrying Miss Ingram – she's your bride!'

'My bride! I have no bride!' he answered. 'But I *will* have one, and you must stay!'

'I *can't* stay!' I cried furiously. 'Do you think I can watch another woman become your bride? Do you think I'm a machine, without feelings? Do you think, because I'm small and poor and plain, that I have no soul and no heart? Well, you're wrong! I have as much soul and heart as you. It is my spirit that speaks to your spirit! We are equal in the sight of God!'

'We are!' repeated Mr Rochester, taking me in his arms and kissing me. 'Don't struggle, Jane, like a wild restless bird!'

'Let me go, Mr Rochester. I am no bird, but a free human being,' and I managed to break away.

'Yes, Jane, you are free to decide. I ask you to walk through life with me, to be my constant companion.'

'You're laughing at me. You've already chosen your companion for life.' I was crying quietly, while Mr Rochester looked gently and seriously at me.

'Jane,' he said, 'I ask you to be my wife. You are my equal, Jane. Will you marry me? Don't you believe me?'

'Not at all,' I answered.

'I'll convince you! Listen, I don't love Miss Ingram and she doesn't love me. She only liked me for my wealth, and when I, disguised as the gipsy woman, told her that I had only a little money, she and her mother lost interest in me. You strange magical spirit,

I love *you*! You, small and poor and plain, I ask *you* to marry me!'

'You want to marry *me*?' I cried, almost beginning to believe him. 'But I have no friends, no money, no family!'

'I don't care, Jane! Say yes, quickly! It's cruel to make me suffer like this! Give me my name, say, "Edward, I'll marry you!" ' he cried, his face very pale in the moonlight.

'Are you serious? Do you really love me? Do you honestly want me to be your wife?' I asked.

'I swear it.'

'Then, Edward, I will marry you.'

'My little wife!' He held me in his arms for a long time, kissing me gently. Once he murmured, 'No family! That's good. No family to interfere!' and then, 'I don't care what people think!' and again and again, 'Are you happy, Jane?' I thought of nothing except the great happiness of being with him for ever.

But while we were talking the weather had changed. A strong wind was now blowing and there was a loud crack of thunder. Suddenly rain poured down, and although we hurried back to the house, we were quite wet when we arrived in the hall. We did not notice Mrs Fairfax standing in the shadows.

'Good night, my darling,' he said, kissing me repeatedly. As I ran upstairs, I caught sight of the old lady's shocked face.

'Tomorrow I'll explain to her,' I thought. Just then I was too happy to think about anything except our bright future.

Outside, the storm continued furiously all night, and in the morning we discovered that the great tree at the bottom of the garden, which had stood for hundreds of years, had been hit by lightning and torn in half.

16

Preparing for the wedding

I was a little nervous before seeing Mr Rochester next morning. Was I really going to marry him, or was it all a dream? But I soon felt calmer when he came to meet me and kissed me.

'Jane, you look well and smiling and pretty,' he said. 'You will be Jane Rochester in four weeks' time, not a day more. I'll send for my family jewels, which are kept in a London bank. They are for my bride, whether she's a great lady or a governess.'

'Oh no, sir!' I cried. 'I'm too plain for jewels! I'm not used to wearing them.'

'I insist, Jane. Today I'm taking you in the carriage to Millcote to buy you some elegant clothes. In a month's time we'll have a quiet wedding in the local church, and after a few days in London we'll travel through all the countries of Europe.'

'Well, sir, you seem very eager to please me, but I wonder if you will agree to a request of mine.'

'Ask me anything, Jane, anything!'

'Indeed I will. This is my request. I ask you *not* to give me jewels and fine clothes.'

'If that's really your wish, I agree. But can't you think of anything I can give you?'

'Well, I'd like you to give me the answer to a question.'

He looked worried, and turned away from me.

'Curiosity is dangerous,' he said. 'I may not be able to agree to this particular request. Well, what is it?'

'How stern you look! I suppose that's how you will look when we are married! This is what I want to know. Why did you take such trouble to make me believe you wished to marry Miss Ingram?'

He stopped frowning at once and smiled down at me.

'Is that all? What a relief! All right, I shall have to confess, although you may be angry with me, Jane – as angry as you were last night, when you told me we were equal. Well, I pretended to love Miss Ingram to make you madly jealous. I wanted you to be as much in love with me as I was with you.'

'And I suppose you didn't care at all about poor Miss Ingram's feelings?'

'She only has one feeling – pride. *Were* you jealous, Jane?'

'Never mind, Mr Rochester. One more request – please explain everything to Mrs Fairfax. She looked so shocked last night!'

When I visited the old housekeeper later that day, I found she was amazed by the news that I was going to marry the master.

'I would never have thought it!' she kept repeating. 'Mr Rochester, so proud and such a gentleman! To marry his governess!' She examined me closely, as if to discover the reason for this strange event, and shook her head, still puzzled. 'He's twenty years older than you! He could be your father!'

'No, indeed, Mrs Fairfax,' I replied crossly. 'He looks much younger than that!'

'Is he really going to marry you for love?' she asked.

I was so hurt by her amazement that tears came to my eyes.

'Why?' I asked. 'Do you think he couldn't possibly love me?'

'No, no, Miss Eyre, but you must realize that this is a very unusual situation. You must be careful of your reputation. I advise you to keep him at a distance until you are married.'

Although I was upset by the old lady's words, I followed her advice, and in the weeks before the wedding I went on teaching Adèle as usual. Only in the evenings did I spend some time with Mr Rochester, and I was careful not to allow him to hold me in his arms or kiss me. Sometimes he was angry with me and called me a 'hard little thing' or 'a cruel spirit', but I preferred that to being called 'my darling'. I saw that Mrs Fairfax approved of my correct behaviour, and I knew that he respected me for it. But it was not easy for me.

I would rather have shown him my love. My future husband was becoming my whole world, and more than that, my hope of heaven.

At last the night before the wedding arrived. My clothes were packed and I was ready. But I was anxious to see Mr Rochester, who had been away on business, so I ran out of the quiet house to meet him on the road. A wild, stormy wind was blowing, and in the garden I passed the wreck of the great tree. Then suddenly I saw him riding towards me.

'You see!' he shouted. 'You can't do without me! Jump up on to my horse!' Together we rode back to Thornfield. While he ate dinner, I sat quietly beside him. He looked closely at me.

'You look sad, Jane,' he said. 'Is anything wrong? Are you nervous about your new life?'

'No,' I replied firmly. 'I'm not worried about that, because I love you. But last night I had a strange dream, a terrible dream! It was dark and windy outside, and before I went to sleep I could hear a dog growling in the distance. In my dream I was carrying a small child in my arms down a long road. I was trying to catch up with you, but I couldn't.'

'And you still worry about a foolish dream, when I'm close to you? But say you love me again, Jane.'

'I do love you, Edward. But I haven't finished my story.'

'Is there more? Well, go on.'

'I dreamed that Thornfield was totally destroyed, just a heap of stones. I was still carrying the child, but now I could see you riding away into the distance. I knew you would never come back! Then I woke up.'

'That's all then, Jane. Nothing to worry about.'

'No, wait. There was candle-light in my room, and a strange shape examining the wedding dress hanging in my cupboard. My blood ran cold. It wasn't Mrs Fairfax or any of the servants, it wasn't even Grace Poole. It was a horrible sight!'

'Describe the shape, Jane.'

'It looked like a tall woman, with long thick dark hair hanging down. She took up the beautiful veil you bought me, put it on her own head, then turned to admire herself in the mirror. It was then that I saw her wild, inhuman face! She removed the veil, tore it in two and threw it on the floor.'

'And then?' Mr Rochester seemed almost nervous.

'She came to my bedside, put her candle close to my face and stared fiercely at me. I must have fainted, and I suppose she left. Now can you tell me who or what that woman was?'

'Jane, you are too sensitive. That was just a dream. Don't think about it any more!' he answered comfortingly.

'That's just what I said to myself when I woke up this morning, but when I looked on the floor, there was the veil, torn in two halves!' I felt Mr Rochester suddenly tremble.

'To think what might have happened!' he cried, throwing his arms around me. 'Thank God it was only the veil!' After a few moments he said calmly, 'Now, Jane, be sensible. That woman must have been Grace Poole. There is no other explanation.'

'Perhaps you're right,' I admitted slowly.

'One day I'll explain to you why I keep her in my house. But tonight, go and sleep in Adèle's room. You'll be quite safe there. Just dream about our future!'

17

The wedding day

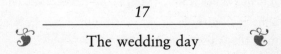

We had no friends or family to accompany us to the church. I had not told my Reed cousins about our wedding, but I had written to my uncle, John Eyre, in Madeira. Mr

Rochester was in such a hurry that he only allowed me a short time to put on my wedding dress and veil.

'Jane, you look lovely,' he said. 'But you can only have ten minutes for breakfast!' We almost ran up the road to the church, his strong hand holding mine. His dark face looked stern, and he did not speak. I did not notice the weather or my surroundings at all, I only wanted to know why he looked so fierce. Suddenly he noticed how pale I was, and stopped for a moment to let me get my breath back. Then we walked more slowly into the church.

The priest and the clerk were waiting for us. There was nobody else except two strangers who were standing at the back of the church. The ceremony began, and soon I heard the priest come to the point in the wedding where he had to ask, 'Is there any reason why these two people should not be married?'

The priest paused for a second, as was the custom, but before he could continue, a voice from the back of the church said clearly,

'There *is* a reason.'

The priest looked up from his book, and stood silent. Mr Rochester said in his deep voice, without turning his head, 'Continue with the ceremony.'

Silence fell again. Then the priest shook his head. 'I must investigate this first,' he said. One of the strangers from the back of the church came forward and said, calmly and quietly,

'This wedding cannot continue, because Mr Rochester is already married.'

I felt as if I had been hit. Mr Rochester's whole face was like colourless marble. Without speaking or smiling, he was holding me tightly round the waist, as if he would never let go.

'Who are you?' he growled at the stranger. 'And tell me what you know of this supposed wife of mine.'

'I'm a lawyer, sir. I have a certificate here proving that you married Bertha Mason in the West Indies fifteen years ago.'

'That may prove I've been married, but it doesn't prove that she's still alive.'

'I can produce a witness,' said the lawyer, 'who has seen her alive recently.'

'Produce him – or go to hell!' said Mr Rochester.

'Here he is. Mr Mason!' called the lawyer. And the second stranger slowly approached from the shadows, his pale face looking frightened. Mr Rochester, staring furiously at him, raised his strong right arm to knock him down.

'No!' cried Mason, trembling. Mr Rochester dropped his arm, and turned away in disgust.

'Sir,' said the priest, frowning, 'don't forget we are in the house of God. Mr Mason, please tell us if this gentleman's wife is still alive.'

'Produce your witness – or go to hell!' said Mr Rochester.

'She's at Thornfield Hall,' replied Mason in a weak voice. 'I'm her brother and I've seen her there.'

'Thornfield Hall!' cried the priest. 'I've lived here for years, and I've never heard of a Mrs Rochester!'

'I was careful to keep her a secret,' murmured Mr Rochester, frowning. After a few minutes' thought, he announced, 'I must reveal the truth, I suppose. There will be no wedding today. No doubt God will punish me for this. What this lawyer says is true. I've been married, and my wife still lives! I was tricked into marrying her when I was young, in the West Indies. Madness runs in her family, but they didn't tell me that. Now she's more of an animal than a woman. I keep her locked away, guarded by my old servant Grace Poole. I invite you all to come to my house to see her, and to judge whether I had the right to ask this innocent young girl to marry me. Follow me!'

Still holding me firmly, he left the church, followed by the others. At the door of Thornfield Hall, Mrs Fairfax, Adèle and the servants rushed forward, smiling, to congratulate us.

'Too late!' cried the master, waving them away. 'Your congratulations are fifteen years too late!' We all went up to the top floor, and entered the room where Mason had been attacked. Mr Rochester lifted the curtain, opened the secret door and showed us the little room. Grace Poole was making soup over a fire, and behind her a shape crawled on the floor. It was hard to say whether it was animal or human. It growled like a wild animal, but it wore clothes, and had long, thick, dark hair.

'How are you, Mrs Poole?' asked the master. 'And how is your patient today?'

'Not bad, sir,' answered Grace, 'but be careful. She'll try and bite you if she sees you, sir.' Just then the shape turned and with a fierce cry attacked Mr Rochester violently. I recognized her dark, ugly face. They struggled for a moment, and then he held her down and, with Mrs Poole's help, tied her to a chair. He turned to the others with a bitter smile.

'You see, gentlemen, this is *my wife*. This is the partner I have to live with for ever. And instead I wished to have *this*' (laying his hand on my shoulder) '. . . this young girl. Can you honestly blame me? Compare the two, and then judge me!'

We all left the room silently. As we went downstairs the lawyer said to me, 'I know you weren't aware of this, Miss Eyre. Nobody will blame you, and Mr Mason will tell your uncle so, when he goes back to Madeira.'

'My uncle! Do you know him?' I asked, surprised.

'I'm his lawyer. Mr Mason and he have often done business together. On his way back to the West Indies, Mr Mason stopped

'*You see, gentlemen, this is* my wife.'

in Madeira and stayed with Mr Eyre, who mentioned that his niece was going to marry a Mr Rochester.'

'Yes, I wrote to tell him I was getting married,' I said.

'Well, when Mr Mason explained that Mr Rochester was already married, your uncle sent him straight back to England to prevent you from marrying and making a terrible mistake. I'm afraid your uncle is very ill and will probably die soon, so I think you had better stay in England, until you receive further news of him.'

After the gentlemen had left, I entered my room and locked the door. Slowly I took off my wedding dress and veil. I was weak and exhausted, and only just beginning to realize what had happened. Could I ever again trust the being I had turned into a sort of god? I would not think of him as evil, but he could not have felt *real* love for me. How foolish I had been to believe him, and love him so much! My hopes were all dead, and my future was empty. I lay on my bed, faint and wishing for death, while darkness swam around me.

18

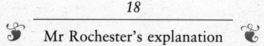

Mr Rochester's explanation

Sometime in the afternoon I recovered a little, but I felt faint as I stood up, and realized I had not eaten anything all day. So I opened my bedroom door and almost fell over Mr Rochester, who was sitting in a chair just outside.

'I've been waiting for you all this time, Jane,' he said. 'And I haven't heard you scream or shout or cry. Aren't you angry with me? I never meant to hurt you. Will you ever forgive me?'

He sounded so sincere that I forgave him at once in my heart.

'Scold me, Jane! Tell me how wicked I am!' he said.

'Sir, I can't. I feel tired and weak. I want some water.'

He took me in his arms and carried me downstairs to the library, where he put me in front of the fire, and gave me a glass of wine. I began to feel better. He bent to kiss me, but I turned my face determinedly away.

'What!' he cried. 'You refuse to kiss me! Because I'm Bertha Mason's husband? Is that it?'

'Yes, sir.'

'I know you very well, Jane. I know how firm you are when you've decided something. You're planning to destroy my hope of happiness. You intend to be a stranger to me from now on. And if I'm friendly towards you in future, you'll remind yourself, "That man nearly made me his mistress – I must be ice-cold to him," and ice-cold is what you'll be.'

'It's true, sir,' I said, trying to stop my voice from trembling, 'that everything around me has changed, so I must change too. Adèle must have a new governess.'

'Oh, Adèle will go to boarding school. I've already decided that. And you and I will both leave this house, this narrow stone hell, this house of living death. We can never be happy here, under the same roof as that woman. Oh, I hate her!'

'You shouldn't hate her, sir,' I said. 'It's not her fault she's mad, poor thing.'

'Jane, my darling, it's not because she's mad that I hate her. If you were mad, I wouldn't hate you. I'd look after you lovingly. But why talk of madness? We are all ready to travel, everything is packed. Tomorrow we'll leave. I have a place to go to, where nobody will find us or talk about us—'

'And take Adèle with you, sir, she'll be a companion for you,' I interrupted. I knew I had to tell him soon.

'Adèle? What do you mean, Jane? She's going to school. I don't want her, I want *you* with me. Do you understand?'

I did, but I slowly shook my head. He was becoming angry, and was staring fiercely at me. He looked as if he was about to lose control. I was not at all afraid, because I knew I still had the power to calm him. So I took his hand and stroked it, saying,

'Sit down, sir, I'll talk or listen to you as long as you like.' I had been struggling with tears for some time and now I let them flow freely. It was a great relief.

'Don't cry, Jane, please be calm,' he begged.

'How can I be calm when you're so angry?'

'I'm not angry, but I love you so much, and your pale little face looked so stern and decided.' He tried to put his arm round me, but I would not let him.

'Jane!' he said sadly, 'you don't love me, then?'

'I *do* love you,' I answered, 'more than ever, but this is the last time I can say it. There is only one thing for me to do, but you'll be furious if I mention it.'

'Oh, mention it! If I'm angry, you can always burst into tears,' he said, with a half-smile.

'Mr Rochester, I must leave you. I must start a new life among strangers.'

'Of course. I told you we would leave. I'll ignore that nonsense about *you* leaving *me*. You'll be Mrs Rochester and I'll be your husband until I die. We'll live happily and innocently together in a little white house I have in the south of France. Jane, don't shake your head, or I'll get angry.'

'Sir, your wife is alive,' I dared to say, although he was looking aggressively at me, 'and if I lived with you like that, I'd be your mistress.'

'I'm a fool!' he said suddenly. 'I haven't told you the whole story! Oh, I'm sure you'll agree when you know everything! Listen, Jane, you know that my father loved money very much?'

'I heard someone say that, yes, sir.'

'Well, he hated the idea of dividing the family property, so he left it all to my elder brother. But that meant I would be poor unless I married a rich wife, so he decided I should marry Bertha Mason, the daughter of his wealthy friend Jonas Mason. I was young and easily impressed, so when I saw her in the West Indies, beautiful and elegantly dressed, I thought I loved her. What a fool I was then! After the wedding I learned that my bride's mother and younger brother were both mad. Dick Mason will probably be in the same state one day. My father knew all this, but did not tell me. I soon found that Bertha and I had nothing in common. Not only was she coarse and stupid, her madness also made her violent. I lived with her for four years. By now my father and brother were dead, so I was rich, but I considered myself poor, because I was tied to a mad wife until death.'

'I pity you, sir, I do pity you.'

'Pity, Jane, is an insult from some people, but from you I accept it as the mother of love. Well, I had moments of despair when I intended to shoot myself, but in the end I decided to bring the mad woman back to Thornfield Hall, where nobody knew that we were married. She has lived here ever since. Even Mrs Fairfax and the servants don't know the whole truth about her. But although I pay Grace Poole well, and trust her absolutely, she sometimes drinks too much and allows the creature to escape. Twice she has got out of her room at night, as you know. The first time she nearly burnt me in my bed, and the second time she visited you, and must have been reminded of her own wedding day by seeing your wedding dress.'

'And what did you do, sir, when you had brought her here?'

'I travelled all over Europe, Jane. I was looking for a good and intelligent woman to love—'

'But you couldn't marry, sir,' I interrupted.

'I believed I could. I thought I might find some reasonable woman who would understand my case and accept me.'

'Well, sir, did you?'

'Not in Europe, Jane, where I spent ten long years looking for an ideal. I tried taking mistresses, like Céline, the French dancer. But finally, bitter and disappointed with my wasted life, I returned to Thornfield on a frosty winter afternoon. And when my horse slipped and fell on the ice, a little figure appeared and insisted on helping me. In the weeks that followed, I began to depend on that bird-like little figure for my happiness and new interest in life.'

'Don't talk any more of the past, sir,' I said, wiping a secret tear from my eye.

'No, Jane, you're right, the future is much brighter. You understand now, don't you? I've wasted half my life in misery and loneliness, but now I've found you. You are at the centre of my heart. It was stupid of me to try to marry you like that without explaining. I should have confessed everything, as I do now, and appealed to your great generosity of spirit. I promise to love you and stay with you for ever. Jane, promise me the same.'

A pause. 'Why are you silent, Jane?'

This was a terrible moment for me. In the struggle and confusion that was going on in my heart I knew that he loved me and I loved him, but I also knew that I must leave him!

'Jane, just promise me, "I will be yours".'

'Mr Rochester, I will *not* be yours.' Another pause.

'Jane,' he said, with a gentleness that cut into my soul, 'Jane, do you intend us to live apart for ever?'

'I do.'

'Jane,' (bending towards me and kissing me), 'is that still your intention?'

'It is,' I replied, pulling away from him.

'Oh Jane, this is a bitter shock. It would not be wicked to love me.'

'It would be wicked to do what you want.'

'Jane, just imagine my horrible life when you have gone. I shall be alone with that mad woman upstairs. Where shall I find friendship, and hope?'

'You can only trust in God and yourself. Live without doing wrong, and die hoping to go to heaven.'

'That's impossible without you! And . . . and you have no family to offend by living with me!' He was beginning to sound desperate. I knew that what he said was true. However, in my heart I also knew I was right to leave.

He seemed to read my thoughts. Rushing furiously across the room, he seized me violently and stared fiercely into my eyes. He could have broken me in two with one hand, but he could not break my spirit. Small and weak as I was, I stared firmly back at him.

'Your eyes, Jane,' he said, 'are the eyes of a bird, a free, wild being. Even if I break your cage, I can't reach you, beautiful creature! You'll fly away from me. But you could choose to fly to me! Come, Jane, come!' He let me go, and only looked at me. How hard it was to resist that look!

'I am going,' I said.

'Does my deep love mean nothing to you? Oh Jane, my hope . . . my love . . . my life!' and he threw himself despairingly on the sofa. I had reached the door, but I could not leave. I walked back, bent over him, and kissed his cheek.

'Goodbye, my dear master!' I said. 'May God protect you!'

'Without your love, Jane, my heart is broken,' he said. 'But perhaps you will, so generously, give me your love after all—' He jumped up with hope in his eyes, holding out his arms to me. But I turned and ran out of the room.

That night I only slept a little, dreaming of the red room at Gateshead. The moonlight shone into my bedroom, as it did then, and I saw a vision on the ceiling, a white figure looking down on me. It seemed to whisper to my spirit: 'Daughter, leave now before you are tempted to stay.'

'Mother, I will,' I answered. And when I woke up, although it was still dark outside, I wrapped up some spare clothes in a parcel, and put a little money in a purse. As I crept downstairs, I could hear Mr Rochester in his room, walking up and down and sighing. I could find heaven in this room if I wanted. I just had to enter and say, 'I will love you and live with you through life until death!' My hand moved towards the handle. But I stopped myself, and went miserably downstairs and out of the house.

Setting out on the road, I could not help thinking of Mr Rochester's despair when he found himself abandoned. I hated myself for wounding him, and for perhaps driving him to a life of wickedness, or even death. I wanted desperately to be with him, to comfort him, but somehow I made myself keep walking, and when a coach passed, I arranged to travel on it as far as my money would pay for. Inside the coach I cried the bitterest tears of my life.

19

Finding shelter

I was put down at Whitcross, a crossroads on the moor, after travelling for two days in the coach. As it rolled away, I realized I had left my parcel inside, and given the coachman all the coins in my purse. I was alone on the open moor, with no money or possessions. Lonely white roads stretched across the great, wide moors as far as the hills. I was glad to see there were no towns here, because I did not want people to question me or pity me. So I walked across the moor, until I found a dry place to sleep, in the shelter of a small hill. Luckily it was a warm night, with no rain. The next day was hot and sunny, but I needed food and water, so I could not stay on the moor.

Taking one of the white roads, I eventually found a small village. I needed all my courage to knock on some of the doors, asking if there was any paid work I could do. None of the village people could help me, and I could not bring myself to beg for food, although by now I felt weak and faint. At the baker's I offered to exchange my leather gloves for a small cake, but the baker's wife looked at my dirty clothes and said, 'I'm sorry, but how do I know you haven't stolen them?' All I ate that day was a piece of bread, which I begged from a farmer eating his supper. I spent another night on the moor, but this time the air was cold and the ground was damp. Next day I walked from house to house again, looking in vain for work. I was now very weak from lack of food, and I began to wonder why I should struggle to stay alive, when I did not want to live.

It was getting dark again, and I was alone on the moor. In the distance I could see a faint light, and I decided to try to reach it.

I was alone on the moor, and now very weak from lack of food.

The wind and rain beat down on me, and I fell down several times, but finally I arrived at a long, low house, standing rather isolated in the middle of the moor. Hiding near the door, I could just see into the kitchen through a small uncurtained window. There was an elderly woman, who might be the housekeeper, mending clothes, and two young ladies, who seemed to be learning a language with dictionaries. The kitchen looked so clean and bright, and the ladies so kind and sensible, that I dared to knock at the door. The elderly woman opened it, but she must have thought I was a thief or a beggar, because she refused to let me speak to the young ladies. The door closed firmly, shutting me out from the warmth inside.

I dropped on to the wet doorstep, worn out and hopeless, prepared to die. There the young ladies' brother found me, when he returned home a few minutes later, and he insisted, much against the housekeeper's wishes, on bringing me into the house. They gave me bread and milk, and asked my name.

'Jane Elliott,' I replied. I did not want anybody to know where I had come from. To their further questions I answered that I was too tired to speak. Finally they helped me upstairs to a bedroom, and I sank gratefully into a warm, dry bed.

For three days and nights I lay in bed, exhausted by my experiences, and hardly conscious of my surroundings. As I was recovering, Hannah, the housekeeper, came to sit with me, and told me all about the family. She had known them since they were babies. Their mother had been dead for years, and their father had died only three weeks before. The girls, Diana and Mary Rivers, had to work as governesses, as their father had lost a lot of money in business. St John, their brother, was the vicar in the nearest village, Morton. They only used this house, called Moor House, in the holidays.

When I felt strong enough to get dressed and go downstairs, Diana and Mary looked after me very kindly, and made me feel welcome in their pleasant home. Their brother, however, seemed stern and cold. He was between twenty-eight and thirty, fair-haired and extremely handsome. Diana and Mary were curious about my past, but sensitive enough to avoid asking questions which would hurt me. St John, on the other hand, made determined efforts to discover who I was, but I, just as firmly, refused to explain more than necessary. I told them only that, after attending Lowood school, I became a governess in a wealthy family, where an unfortunate event, not in any way my fault, caused me to run away. That was all I was prepared to say. I offered to do any kind of work, teaching, sewing, cleaning, so that I could become independent again. St John approved of my keenness to work, and promised to find me some paid employment.

20

A new home

I spent a month at Moor House, in an atmosphere of warm friendship. I learned to love what Diana and Mary loved – the little old grey house, the wild open moors around it, and the lonely hills and valleys where we walked for hours. I read the books they read, and we discussed them eagerly. Diana started teaching me German, and I helped Mary to improve her drawing. We three shared the same interests and opinions, and spent the days and evenings very happily together.

However, St John hardly ever joined in our activities. He was often away from home, visiting the poor and the sick in Morton. His strong sense of duty made him insist on going, even if the weather was very bad. But despite his hard work I thought he lacked true happiness and peace of mind. He often stopped reading or writing to stare into the distance, dreaming perhaps of some ambitious plan. Once I heard him speak at a church service in Morton, and although he was an excellent speaker, there was a certain bitterness and disappointment in his words. He was clearly not satisfied with his present life.

The holiday was coming to an end. Soon Diana and Mary would leave Moor House to return to the wealthy families in the south, where they were both governesses, and St John would go back to the vicar's house in Morton, with Hannah, his housekeeper. Although his cold manner made it difficult for me to talk to him, I had to ask him whether he had found any employment for me.

'I have,' he answered slowly, 'but remember I am only a poor country vicar, and can't offer you a job with a high salary, so you may not wish to accept it. There's already a school for boys in Morton, and now I want to open one for girls, so I've rented a building for it, with a small cottage for the schoolteacher. Miss Oliver, who lives in the area and is the only daughter of a rich factory-owner, has kindly paid for the furniture. Will you be the schoolteacher? You would live in the cottage rent-free, and receive thirty pounds a year, no more.'

I thought about it for a moment. It was not as good as being a governess in an important family, but at least I would have no master. I would be free and independent.

'Thank you, Mr Rivers, I accept gladly,' I replied.

'But you do understand?' he asked, a little worried. 'It will only be a village school. The girls will be poor and uneducated. You'll be teaching reading, writing, counting, sewing, that's all. There'll be no music or languages or painting.'

'I understand, and I'll be happy to do it,' I answered.

He smiled, well satisfied with me.

'And I'll open the school tomorrow, if you like,' I added.

'Very good,' he agreed. Then looking at me, he said, 'But I don't think you'll stay long in the village.'

'Why not? I'm not ambitious, although I think *you* are.'

He looked surprised. 'I know I am, but how did you discover that? No, I think you won't be satisfied by living alone. You need people to make you happy.' He said no more.

Diana and Mary lost their usual cheerfulness as the moment for leaving their home and their brother came closer.

'You see, Jane,' Diana explained, 'St John is planning to become a missionary very soon. He feels his purpose in life is to spread the Christian religion in unexplored places where the people have never heard the word of God. So we won't see him for many years, perhaps never again! He looks quiet, Jane, but he's very determined. I know he's doing God's work, but it will break my heart to see him leave!' and she broke down in tears.

Mary wiped her own tears away, as she said, 'We've lost our father. Soon we'll lose our brother too!'

Just then St John himself entered, reading a letter. 'Our uncle John is dead,' he announced. The sisters did not look shocked or sad, but seemed to be waiting for more information. St John gave them the letter to read, and then they all looked at each other, smiling rather tiredly.

'Well,' said Diana, 'at least we have enough money to live on. We don't really need any more.'

'Yes,' said St John, 'but unfortunately we can imagine how different our lives might have been.' He went out. There was a silence for a few minutes, then Diana turned to me.

'Jane, you must be surprised that we don't show any sadness at our uncle's death. I must explain. We've never met him. He was my mother's brother, and he and my father quarrelled years ago about a business deal. That's when my father lost most of his money. My uncle, on the other hand, made a fortune of twenty thousand pounds. As he never married and had no relations apart from us and one other person, my father always hoped we would inherit uncle John's money. But it seems this other relation has inherited his whole fortune. Of course we shouldn't have expected anything, but Mary and I would have felt rich with only a thousand pounds each, and St John would have been able to help so many more poor people!' She said no more, and none of us referred to the subject again that evening.

The next day the Rivers family returned to their separate places of work, and I moved to the cottage in Morton.

21

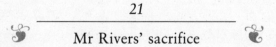

Mr Rivers' sacrifice

I had twenty village girls to teach, some of them with such a strong country accent that I could hardly communicate with them. Only three could read, and none could write, so at the end of my first day I felt quite depressed at the thought of the hard work ahead of me. But I reminded myself that I was fortunate to have any sort of job, and that I would certainly get used to teaching these girls, who, although they were very poor, might be as good and as intelligent as children from the greatest families in England.

Ever since I ran away from Thornfield, Mr Rochester had remained in my thoughts, and now, as I stood at my cottage door that first evening, looking at the quiet fields, I allowed myself to imagine again the life I could have had with him in his little white house in the south of France. He would have loved me, oh yes, he would have loved me very much for a while. 'He *did* love me,' I thought, 'nobody will ever love me like that again.' But then I told myself that I would only have been his mistress, in a foreign country, and for a short time, until he grew tired of me. I should be much happier here as a schoolteacher, free and honest, in the healthy heart of England. But strangely enough, St John Rivers found me crying as he approached the cottage. Frowning at the sight of the tears on my cheeks, he asked me,

'Do you regret accepting this job, then?'

'Oh no,' I replied quickly, 'I'm sure I'll get used to it soon. And I'm really very grateful to have a home, and work to do. After all, I had nothing a few weeks ago.'

'But you feel lonely, perhaps?' he asked, still puzzled.

'I haven't had time to feel lonely yet.'

'Well, I advise you to work hard, and not to look back into your past. If something which we know is wrong tempts us, then we must make every effort to avoid it, by putting our energy to better use. A year ago I too was very miserable, because I was bored by the routine life of a country vicar, and I was tempted to change my profession. But suddenly there was light in my darkness, and God called me to be a missionary. No profession could be greater than that! Since that moment of truth, I have been perfectly happy, making my preparations for leaving England and going abroad in the service of God. Happy, that is, except for one little human weakness, which I have sworn to overcome.'

His eyes shone as he spoke of his great purpose in life, and I was listening, fascinated, so neither of us heard the light footsteps approaching the cottage along the grassy path.

'Good evening, Mr Rivers,' said a charming voice, as sweet as a bell. St John jumped as if hit between the shoulders, then turned slowly and stiffly to face the speaker. A vision in white, with a young, girlish figure, was standing beside him. When she threw back her veil, she revealed a face of perfect beauty. St John glanced quickly at her, but dared not look at her for long. He kept his eyes on the ground as he answered, 'A lovely evening, but it's late for you to be out alone.'

'Oh, Father told me you'd opened the new girls' school, so I simply had to come to meet the new schoolteacher. That must be you,' she said to me, smiling. 'Do you like Morton? And your pupils? And your cottage?' I realized this must be the rich Miss Oliver who had generously furnished my cottage.

'Yes, indeed, Miss Oliver,' I replied. 'I'm sure I'll enjoy teaching here. And I like my cottage very much.'

'I'll come and help you teach sometimes. I get so bored at home! Mr Rivers, I've been away visiting friends, you know. I've had such fun! I was dancing with the officers until two o'clock this morning! They're all so charming!'

St John's face looked sterner than usual and his lip curled in disapproval, as he lifted his handsome head and looked straight into Miss Oliver's laughing eyes. He breathed deeply and his chest rose, as if his heart wanted to fly out of its cage, but he said nothing, and after a pause Miss Oliver continued, 'Do come and visit my father, Mr Rivers. Why don't you ever come?'

'I can't come, Miss Rosamund.' It seemed clear to me that St John had to struggle with himself to refuse this smiling invitation.

'Well, if you don't want to, I must go home then. Goodbye!' She held out her hand. He just touched it, his hand trembling.

'Goodbye!' he said in a low, hollow voice, his face as white as a sheet. They walked away in different directions. She turned back twice to look at him, but he did not turn round at all.

The sight of another person's suffering and sacrifice stopped me thinking so much about my own problems. I had plenty of opportunities to observe St John and Miss Oliver together. Every day St John taught one Bible lesson at the school, and Miss Oliver, who knew her power over him, always chose that particular moment to arrive at the school door, in her most attractive riding dress. She used to walk past the rows of admiring pupils towards the young vicar, smiling openly at him. He just stared at her, as if he wanted to say, 'I love you, and I know you love me. If I offered you my heart, I think you'd accept. But my heart is already promised as a sacrifice to God.' But he never said anything, and she always turned sadly away like a disappointed child. No doubt he would have given the world to call her back, but he would not give his chance of heaven.

When I discovered that Miss Oliver's father greatly admired the Rivers family, and would have no objection to her marrying a vicar, I decided to try to persuade St John to marry her. I thought he could do more good with Miss Oliver's money in England, than as a missionary under the baking sun in the East.

My chance came some weeks later, when he visited me one November evening in my little cottage. He noticed a sketch I had been doing of Miss Oliver, and could not take his eyes off it.

'I could paint you an exact copy,' I said gently, 'if you admit that you would like it.'

'She's so beautiful!' he murmured, still looking at it. 'I would certainly like to have it.'

'She likes you, I'm sure,' I said, greatly daring, 'and her father respects you. You ought to marry her.'

'It's very pleasant to hear this,' he said, not at all shocked by my honesty. 'I shall allow myself fifteen minutes to think about her.' And he actually put his watch on the table, and sat back in his chair, closing his eyes. 'Married to the lovely Rosamund Oliver! Let me just imagine it! My heart is full of delight!' And there was silence for a quarter of an hour until he picked up his watch, and put the sketch back on the table.

'Temptation has a bitter taste,' he said, shaking his head. 'I can't marry her. You see, although I love her so deeply, I know that Rosamund would not make a good wife for a missionary.'

'But you needn't be a missionary!' I cried.

'Indeed I must! It's the great work God has chosen me to do! I shall carry with me into the darkest corners of the world knowledge, peace, freedom, religion, the hope of heaven! That is what I live for, and what I shall die for!'

'What about Miss Oliver?' I asked after a moment. 'She may be very disappointed if you don't marry her.'

'Miss Oliver will forget me in a month, and will probably marry someone who'll make her far happier than I ever could!'

'You speak calmly, but I know you're suffering.'

'You *are* original,' he said, looking surprised. He had clearly not imagined that men and women could discuss such deep feelings together. 'But believe me, I have overcome this weakness of mine, and become as hard as a rock. My only ambition now is to serve God.' As he picked up his hat before leaving, something on a piece of paper on the table caught his eye. He glanced at me, then tore off a tiny piece very quickly, and with a rapid 'Goodbye!' rushed out of the cottage. I could not imagine what he had found to interest him so much.

22

Sudden wealth

When St John left, it was beginning to snow, and it continued snowing all night and all the next day. In the evening I sat by my fire, listening to the wind blowing outside, and had just started reading when I heard a noise. The wind, I thought, was shaking the door, but no, it was St John, who came in out of the frozen darkness, his coat covered in snow.

'What's happened?' I cried, amazed. 'I thought nobody would be out in weather like this! What's the matter?'

'There's nothing wrong,' he answered calmly, hanging up his coat, and stamping the snow from his boots. 'I just came to have a little talk to you. Besides, since yesterday I've been eager to hear the other half of your story.' He sat down. I had no idea what he was referring to, and remembering his strange behaviour with the piece of paper, I began to fear that he might be going mad. He looked quite normal, however, and we made conversation for a while, although he seemed to be thinking of something else.

Suddenly he said, 'When I arrived I said I wanted to hear the rest of your story. But perhaps it's better if I tell the story. I'm afraid you've heard it before, but listen anyway. Twenty years ago a poor vicar fell in love with a rich man's daughter. She also fell in love with him, and married him, against the advice of all her family. Sadly, less than two years later the couple were both dead. I've seen their grave. Their baby daughter was brought up by an aunt, a Mrs Reed of Gateshead. You jumped – did you hear a noise? I'll continue. I don't know whether the child was happy with Mrs Reed, but she stayed there ten years, until she went to Lowood school, where you were yourself. In fact, it seems her life was quite similar to yours. She became a teacher at Lowood, as you did, and then became a governess in the house of a certain Mr Rochester.'

'Mr Rivers!' I interrupted, unable to keep silent.

'I can imagine how you feel,' he replied, 'but wait till I've finished. I don't know anything about Mr Rochester's character, but I do know that he offered to marry this young girl, who only discovered during the wedding ceremony that he was in fact already married, to a mad woman. The governess disappeared soon after this, and although investigations have been carried out, and advertisements placed in newspapers, and every effort made to find her, nobody knows where she's gone. But she must be found! Mr Briggs, a lawyer, has something very important to tell her.'

'Just tell me one thing,' I said urgently. 'What about Mr Rochester? How and where is he? What's he doing? Is he well?'

'I know nothing about Mr Rochester. Why don't you ask the name of the governess, and why everybody is looking for her?'

'Did Mr Briggs write to Mr Rochester?' I asked.

'He did, but he received an answer not from him, but from the housekeeper, a Mrs Fairfax.'

I felt cold and unhappy. No doubt Mr Rochester had left England for a life of wild pleasure in the cities of Europe. That was what I had been afraid of. Oh, my poor master – once almost my husband – who I had often called 'my dear Edward'!

'As you won't ask the governess's name, I'll tell you myself,' continued St John. 'I've got it written down. It's always better to have facts in black and white.' And he took out of his wallet a tiny piece of paper, which I recognized as part of my sketch book, and showed it to me. On it I read, in my own writing, 'JANE EYRE', which I must have written without thinking.

'The advertisements and Briggs spoke of a Jane Eyre, but I only knew a Jane Elliott,' said St John. 'Are you Jane Eyre?'

'Yes – yes, but doesn't Mr Briggs know anything about Mr Rochester?' I asked desperately.

'I don't think Briggs is at all interested in Mr Rochester. You're forgetting the really important thing. Don't you want to know why he's been looking for you?'

'Well, what did he want?' I asked, almost rudely.

Oh, my poor master – once almost my husband – who I had often called 'my dear Edward'!

'Only to tell you that your uncle, Mr Eyre of Madeira, is dead, that he has left you all his property, and that you're now rich – only that, nothing more.'

Rich! One moment I was poor, the next moment I was wealthy. It was hard to realize my new situation. A fortune brings serious worries and responsibilities with it, which I could hardly imagine. I was sorry to hear that my uncle, my only surviving relation, was dead. However, the inheritance would give me independence for life, and I was glad of that.

'Perhaps you would like to know how much you've inherited?' offered St John politely. 'It's nothing much really, just twenty thousand pounds, I think.'

'Twenty thousand pounds?' The news took my breath away. St John, who I had never heard laugh before, actually laughed out loud at my shocked face. 'Perhaps . . . perhaps you've made a mistake?' I asked him nervously.

'No, there's no mistake. Now I must be leaving. Good night.' He was about to open the door, when suddenly I called, 'Stop! Why did Mr Briggs write to *you* in order to find me?'

'Oh, I'm a vicar. I have ways of discovering things.'

'No, that doesn't satisfy me. Tell me the truth,' I insisted, putting myself between him and the door.

'Well, I'd rather not tell you just now, but I suppose you'll discover it sooner or later. Did you know that my full name is St John Eyre Rivers?'

'No, I didn't! But then what—' And I stopped as light flooded my mind and I saw clearly the chain of circumstances which connected us. But St John continued his explanation.

'My mother's name was Eyre,' he said. 'She had two brothers, one, a vicar, who married Miss Jane Reed of Gateshead, and the other, John Eyre of Madeira. Mr Briggs, Mr Eyre's lawyer, wrote to us telling us that our uncle had died, and left all his property, not to us, because of his quarrel with our father, but to his brother's daughter. Then Mr Briggs wrote again later, saying this girl could not be found. Well, I've found her.' He moved towards the door, his hat in his hand.

'Wait a moment, just let me think,' I said. 'So you, Diana and Mary are my cousins?'

'We are your cousins, yes,' he said, waiting patiently.

As I looked at him, it seemed I had found a brother and sisters to love and be proud of for the rest of my life. The people who had saved my life were my close relations! This was wealth indeed to a lonely heart, brighter and more life-giving than the heavy responsibility of coins and gold.

'Oh, I'm glad – I'm so glad!' I cried, laughing.

St John smiled. 'You were serious when I told you you had inherited a fortune. Now you're excited about something very unimportant.'

'What *can* you mean? It may mean nothing to you. You already have sisters and don't need any more family. But I had nobody, and now I suddenly have three relations in my world, or two, if you don't want to be counted.' I walked rapidly round the room, my thoughts rising so fast I could hardly understand them. The family I now had, the people who had saved me from starvation, I could now help *them*! There were four of us cousins. Twenty thousand pounds, shared equally, would be five thousand pounds each, more than enough for each one of us. It would be a fair and just arrangement, and we would all be happy. I would no longer have the worry of controlling a large amount of money, and they would never have to work again. We would all be able to spend more time together at Moor House.

Naturally, when I made this suggestion to St John and his sisters, they protested strongly, and it was with great difficulty that I finally managed to convince them of my firm intention to carry out this plan. In the end they agreed that it was a fair way of sharing the inheritance, and so the legal steps were taken to transfer equal shares to all of us.

23

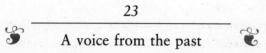

A voice from the past

I promised to stay at Morton school until Christmas, when St John would be able to find another teacher. He was there when I closed the school for the Christmas holidays. I was quite sorry to have to say goodbye to some of my pupils.

'You see what progress they have made! And you've only worked here a few months!' he said. 'Imagine how much more good you could do if you gave your whole life to teaching!'

'Yes,' I answered, 'but I couldn't do it for ever. Don't mention school, I'm on holiday now!'

He looked serious. 'What are your plans?'

'I want you to let me have Hannah for a few days. She and I are going to clean Moor House from top to bottom, and make all the Christmas preparations that you know nothing about, being only a man. Everything must be ready for Diana and Mary when they come home next week, for a really wonderful holiday.'

St John smiled but he was still not satisfied with me. 'That's all right for the moment, but I hope, Jane, that you'll look higher than domestic activity, and think about a better way of using your energy and intelligence in the service of God.'

'St John, I have so many reasons for happiness. I am determined to be happy despite your scolding!'

That week Hannah and I worked harder than we had ever worked in our lives before, but at last all was ready. It was a delight to see Diana's and Mary's faces when they arrived cold and stiff from their long journey, and saw the warm fires and polished furniture, and smelt the cakes and meat dishes cooking.

We three spent the whole of Christmas week in perfect happiness. The air of the moors, the freedom of home, and the beginning of independence made Diana and Mary happier than I had ever seen them. Only St John remained apart from our conversations and laughter. He continued his serious studies, and spent much time visiting the sick as usual.

'Do you still intend to be a missionary?' Diana asked him once, a little sadly.

'Nothing has changed or will change my plans,' he answered. 'I shall leave England in a few months' time.'

'And Rosamund Oliver?' asked Mary gently.

'Rosamund Oliver is engaged to a Mr Granby, a very suitable young man, according to her father.' His face was calm. I realized he had managed to overcome what he called his weakness.

Gradually our life at Moor House lost its holiday feeling, and as we took up our usual habits and regular studies again, St John sat with us more often. Sometimes I had the impression he was observing us. One day, when Diana and Mary were out and I was learning German, he suddenly said to me, 'I want you to learn Hindustani instead of German. I'll need it for my missionary work in India, and you could help me to learn it by studying with me. I've chosen you because I've noticed you have better powers of concentration than either of my sisters.' It seemed so important to him that I could not refuse, and when his sisters returned, they were surprised to find me learning Hindustani with St John.

From now on we spent a lot of time together, studying. I had to work very hard to satisfy him. Under his influence, however, I felt I was losing my freedom to be myself. I could no longer talk or laugh freely, as I knew he only approved of serious moods and studies.

I fell under his freezing spell, obeying all his commands without thinking.

One evening, at bedtime, as he kissed his sisters good night, and was holding out his hand to shake mine, as usual, Diana said, laughing, 'St John! You aren't treating Jane like one of the family! You should kiss her too.' I was rather embarrassed, but St John calmly kissed me, and did so every evening after that.

I had not forgotten Mr Rochester in all these changes of home and fortune. His name was written on my heart, and would stay there as long as I lived. Not only had I written to ask Mr Briggs more about him, I had also written twice to Mrs Fairfax. But after I had waited in vain for six months, I lost hope, and felt low indeed. Diana said I looked ill, and needed a holiday at the seaside, but St John thought I ought to concentrate on more serious work, and gave me even more Hindustani exercises to do.

One day, while he and I were walking on the moors, he announced, 'Jane, I'll be leaving in six weeks.'

'You're doing God's work. He'll protect you,' I replied.

'Yes, it seems strange to me that all my friends don't want to join me. God offers a place in heaven to all who serve Him. What does your heart say to that, Jane?'

'My heart is silent – my heart is silent,' I murmured.

'Then I must speak for it,' said the deep, stern voice. 'Jane, come with me to India as a missionary!'

Was it a call from God? I felt as if I was under a terrible spell, and I trembled, afraid that I might not be able to escape.

'Oh St John, don't choose me!' I begged. But it was useless appealing to a man who always did what he believed to be his duty, however unpleasant it was.

'God intended you to be a missionary's wife,' he continued. 'Trust in Him, Jane. Marry me, for the service of God.'

'I can't do it, St John, I'm not strong enough!' I cried. The iron bars of a cage seemed to be closing in around me.

'I've seen how hard you can work, Jane. You will be a great help to me with Indian women, and in Indian schools.'

I thought, 'Yes, I could do that. But I know that he doesn't love me, and despite that, he asks me to marry him!' So I said,

'I'm ready to go with you to India, but as a sister, not as a wife.'

He shook his head. 'You must see that's impossible. No, a sister could marry at any time, and leave me. I need a wife, who will obey me in life, and who will stay with me until death.'

I trembled as I felt his power over me already. 'I'll give my heart to God,' I said. '*You* don't want it.' As I looked at his stern face, I knew I could go anywhere in the world with him as a colleague, but I could never lose my freedom by marrying him.

'I'll ask you again in a few days' time,' he said, 'and remember, it isn't me you're refusing, but God!'

From then on his manner towards me was as cold as ice, which caused me great pain. I began to understand how, if I were his wife, this good, religious man could soon kill me, without feeling any guilt at all.

When he asked me again, we were alone in the sitting-room. He put his hand on my head and spoke quietly in his deep, sincere voice. 'Remember, Jane, God calls us to work for Him, and will reward us for it. Say you will marry me, and earn your place in heaven!' I admired and respected him, and under his touch my mind was changing. I was tempted to stop struggling against him, as I had been tempted before, in a different way, by Mr Rochester. The missionary gently held my hand. I could resist his anger, but not his gentleness. I desperately wanted to do what was right.

'If I felt certain,' I answered finally, 'that God really wanted me to marry you, I would agree!'

'My prayers are heard!' cried St John. Close together we stood, waiting for a sign from heaven. I was more excited than I had ever been before. There was a total silence in the house, and the room was full of moonlight. Suddenly my heart stopped beating, and I heard a distant voice cry, 'Jane! Jane! Jane!' – nothing more. Where did it come from? It was the voice of Edward Rochester, and it spoke in sadness and in pain.

'I'm coming!' I cried. 'Wait for me!' I ran into the garden calling, 'Where are you?' Only the hills sent a faint echo back.

I broke away from St John, who had followed, asking me questions. It was *my* time to give orders now. I told him to leave me, and he obeyed. In my room I fell to my knees to thank God for the sign he had sent me, and waited eagerly for daylight.

24

Returning to Thornfield

In the morning I explained to Diana and Mary that I had to go on a journey, and would be away for several days. Although they did not know the reason for my journey, they were far too sensitive to my feelings to bother me with questions.

And so I walked to Whitcross, the lonely crossroads on the moor, where I had arrived a year ago with no money or luggage. I took the coach, and after thirty-six hours of travelling I got down at Thornfield village, and almost ran across the fields in my hurry to see the well-known house again, and its owner. I decided to approach from the front, to get the best view of the house. From there I would be able to see my master's window. 'He might even be walking in the gardens,' I thought, 'and I could run to him, touch him! Surely that wouldn't hurt anybody?'

But when I reached the great stone columns of the main gate, I stood still in horror. There, where I had hoped to see a fine, impressive house, was nothing but a blackened heap of stones, with the silence of death about it. No wonder that letters addressed to people here had never received an answer. There must have been a great fire. How had it started? Had any lives been lost? I ran back to the village to find answers to my questions.

'Well, ma'am,' the hotel-owner told me, 'I was one of Mr Rochester's servants at the time, and I can tell you it was his mad wife who started the fire in the governess's room. The master had been wildly in love with the governess, you see, ma'am, although she was just a plain little thing, and when she disappeared, he almost went mad. His wife must have understood enough to be jealous of the girl. Anyway, in the fire the master risked his life helping all the servants out of the house, then bravely went back to save the mad woman. We saw her jump from the roof and fall to her death. But because he went back to help her, he was badly injured in the fire, losing a hand and the sight of both eyes. Very sad, ma'am.'

'Where is he now?' I asked urgently.

'At another house of his, Ferndean Manor, thirty miles away.'

I hired a carriage to drive there at once.

25

Finding Mr Rochester again

Ferndean Manor was a large old house in the middle of a wood. It looked dark and lonely, surrounded by trees. As I approached, the narrow front door opened, and out came a figure I could not fail to recognize, Edward Rochester. I held my breath as I watched, feeling a mixture of happiness and sadness. He looked as strong as before and his hair was still black, but in his face I saw a bitter, desperate look, that I had never seen there before. He walked slowly and hesitatingly along the path. Although he kept looking up eagerly at the sky, it was obvious that he could see nothing. After a while he stopped, and stood quietly there, the rain falling fast on his bent, uncovered head. Finally he found his way painfully back to the house, and closed the door.

When I knocked at the door, Mr Rochester's old servant, John, opened it and recognized me. He and his wife Mary were the only servants their master had wanted to keep when he moved from Thornfield. Although they were surprised to see me, I had no difficulty in arranging to stay at Ferndean that night.

'But he may not want to see you,' warned Mary, as we sat together in the kitchen. 'He refuses to see anybody except us.' She was lighting some candles. 'He always wants candles in the sitting-room when it's dark, even though he's blind.'

'Give them to me, Mary,' I said. 'I'll take them to him.'

The blind man was sitting near the neglected fire in the dark room. 'Put down the candles, Mary,' he sighed.

'Here they are, sir,' I said.

'That *is* Mary, isn't it?' he asked, listening carefully.

'Mary's in the kitchen,' I answered.

'What sweet madness has seized me?' he cried suddenly. 'Where is the speaker? I can't see, but I must feel, or my heart will stop, and my brain will burst! Let me touch you, or I can't live!' I held his wandering hand with both of mine. 'Is it Jane? This is her shape . . .' He released his hand and seized my arm, shoulder, neck, waist and held me close to him.

'She is here,' I said, 'and her heart too. I am Jane Eyre. I've found you and come back to you.'

'My living darling! So you aren't lying dead in a ditch somewhere! Is it a dream? I've dreamed so often of you, only to wake in the morning, abandoned, my life dark, my soul thirsty.'

'I'm alive, and I'm not a dream. In fact, I'm an independent woman now. I've inherited five thousand pounds from my uncle.'

'Ah, that sounds real! I couldn't dream that. But perhaps you have friends now, and don't want to spend much time in a lonely house with a blind man like me.'

'I can do what I like, and I intend to stay with you, unless you object. I'll be your neighbour, your nurse, your housekeeper, your companion. You will never be sad or lonely as long as I live.'

He did not reply immediately, and I was a little embarrassed by his silence. I had assumed he would still want me to be his wife, and wondered why he did not ask me.

'Jane,' he said sadly, 'you cannot always be my nurse. It's kind and generous of you, but you're young, and one day you will want to marry. If I could only see, I'd try to make you love me again, but . . .' and he sighed deeply.

I was very relieved to discover that was all he was worrying about, because I knew that his blindness made no difference at all to my love for him. However, I thought too much excitement was not good for him, so I talked of other things, and made him laugh a little. As we separated at bedtime, he asked me, 'Just one thing, Jane. Were there only ladies in the house where you've been?' I laughed, and escaped upstairs, still laughing. 'A good idea!' I thought. 'A little jealousy will stop him feeling so sorry for himself!'

Next day I took him outside for a long walk in the fresh air. I described the beauty of the fields and sky to him, as we sat close together in the shade of a tree.

'Tell me, Jane, what happened to you when you so cruelly abandoned me?' he asked, holding me tightly in his arms.

And so I told him my story. Naturally he was interested in St John Rivers, my cousin.

'This St John, do you like him?'

'He's a very good man. I couldn't help liking him.'

'He's perhaps a man of fifty or so?'

'St John is only twenty-nine, sir.'

'Rather stupid, I think you said? Not at all intelligent?'

'He has an excellent brain, sir.'

'Did you say he was rather plain, ugly, in fact?'

'St John is a handsome man, tall and fair, with blue eyes.'

Mr Rochester frowned, and swore loudly.

'In fact, sir,' I continued, 'he asked me to marry him.'

'Well, Jane, leave me and go. Oh, until now I thought you would never love another man! But go and marry Rivers!'

'I can never marry him, sir. He doesn't love me, and I don't love him. He's good and great, but as cold as ice. You needn't be jealous, sir. All my heart is yours.'

He kissed me. 'I'm no better than the great tree hit by lightning at Thornfield,' he said. 'I can't expect to have a fresh young plant like you by my side, all my life.'

'You are still strong, sir, and young plants need the strength and safety of a tree to support them.'

'Jane, will you marry me, a poor blind man with one hand, twenty years older than you?'

'Yes, sir.'

'My darling! We'll be married in three days' time, Jane. Thank God! You know I never thought much of religion? Well, lately I've begun to understand that God has been punishing me for my pride and my past wickedness. Last Monday night, in a mood of deep depression, I was sitting by an open window, praying for a little peace and happiness in my dark life. In my heart and soul I wanted you. I cried out "Jane!" three times.'

'Last Monday night, about midnight?' I asked, wondering.

'Yes, but that doesn't matter. *This* is what's really strange. I heard a voice calling "I'm coming, wait for me!" and "Where are you?" And then I heard an echo sent back by hills, but there's no echo here, in the middle of the wood. Jane, you must have been asleep. Your spirit and mine must have met to comfort each other! It was *your* voice I heard!'

I did not tell him I had actually spoken those words many miles away, at that exact moment on that night, because I could hardly understand how it happened myself.

'I thank God!' said Edward Rochester, 'and ask Him to help me live a better life in future!' Together we returned slowly to Ferndean Manor, Edward leaning on my shoulder.

We had a quiet wedding. I wrote to tell the Rivers the news. Diana and Mary wrote back with delighted congratulations, but St John did not reply.

*

Now I have been married for ten years. I know what it is like to love and be loved. No woman has ever been closer to her husband than I am to Edward. I am my husband's life, and he is mine. We are always together, and have never had enough of each other's company. After two years his sight began to return in one eye. Now he can see a little, and when our first child was born and put into his arms, he was able to see that the boy had inherited his fine large black eyes.

Mrs Fairfax is retired, and Adèle has grown into a charming young woman. Diana and Mary are both married, and we visit them once a year. St John achieved his ambition by going to India as planned, and is still there. He writes to me regularly. He is unmarried and will never marry now. He knows that the end of his life is near, but he has no fear of death, and looks forward to gaining his place in heaven.

No woman has ever been closer to her husband than I am to Edward.

Exercises

A Checking your understanding

Chapters 1 – 2 *Write answers to these questions.*
1 What were the names of Jane Eyre's cousins?
2 Who had died in the red room?
3 Who was Jane's only friend at Gateshead?

Chapters 3 – 6 *Are these sentences true (T) or false (F)?*
1 Miss Miller was the headmistress.
2 Helen Burns was punished for her untidiness.
3 Miss Temple told the school that Jane was not a liar.
4 Jane was a teacher at the school for five years.

Chapters 7 – 18 *How much can you remember? Check your answers.*
1 What was the housekeeper's name?
2 Where in the house did Grace Poole work?
3 Who had been Mr Rochester's French mistress?
4 What was the name of the woman expected to marry Mr Rochester?
5 Who killed himself?
6 Who wanted Jane to inherit all his money?
7 Who stopped the wedding?
8 What was the name of Mr Rochester's wife?

Chapters 19 – 23 *Write answers to these questions.*
1 Why did Jane give a false name to the Rivers family?
2 What was St John Rivers' great ambition?
3 What was the sacrifice he had to make?
4 What did Jane do with her inheritance?
5 Why didn't Jane want to marry St John?

Chapters 24 – 25 *Are these sentences true (T) or false (F)?*
1 Grace Poole started the fire which burned down Thornfield.
2 Mr Rochester lost both hands and the sight of one eye.
3 Diana and Mary remained friends of the Rochesters'.
4 Jane and her husband had only one child.

B Working with language

1 *Combine these sentences into longer sentences, using linking words and making any other necessary changes.*
1 Jane was unhappy at school.
2 She found it difficult to accept the strict school rules.
3 Many of the pupils caught typhus fever.
4 Jane remained healthy.
5 She was able to enjoy walking in the fields and valleys.
6 Mr Brocklehurst thought she was an example of evil.
7 Jane had to stand on a chair in the schoolroom as a punishment.
8 She had not done anything wrong.

2 *Choose the best linking word and complete these sentences with information from the story.*
1 Jane would never have attacked John Reed since/if . . . . .
2 Mr Rochester made Jane think he was in love with Blanche Ingram in order to/in case . . . . .
3 As soon as/Before Jane heard of her aunt's illness, she . . . . .
4 The wedding had to be stopped because/although . . . . .
5 As/Although Jane was small and plain, Mr Rochester . . . . .

C Activities

1 Write a letter to the author of the book, giving a critical view of it.
2 Write Jane's letter to the Rivers family, explaining that she had married Mr Rochester.
3 How do you think Jane's childhood experiences affected her character and later life?

Glossary

basin a container for water for washing hands and face

bear to suffer pain or unhappiness

Bible the holy book of the Christian religion

biscuit a flat, thin, dry cake

boarding school a school where pupils live

bully *(n)* a person who hurts or frightens weaker people on purpose; *(v)* to act like a bully

charity giving money, help, etc. to people in need (e.g. in the old days to a school for poor children)

Christian a person who believes in the teachings of Jesus Christ

churchyard ground near or belonging to a church, where dead members of that church are buried

coachman a driver of a horse-drawn carriage or coach

darling used when speaking to someone you love

elegant fashionable and graceful in appearance and clothes

evil *(adj)* not good, wicked; *(n)* great wickedness

fair *(adj)* just, honest, right according to the rules

firm *(adj)* strong and determined in attitude and behaviour

furious very angry in an uncontrolled way

gentleman a man of good family, usually wealthy

gipsy a member of a race of travelling people

governess a female teacher who lives with a wealthy family and educates their children at home

groan to make a low sound in pain or suffering

Hindustani the main language in India

housekeeper a person employed to manage a house

lean *(v)* to support or rest oneself in a bent position

liar a person who tells lies

library a room in a house used for reading

love-affair a sexual relationship between a man and a woman

maid a female servant; **housemaid** a maid who does general housework

ma'am a short form for madam

marble a white or coloured stone, hard and cold to touch

master a male employer, the man in control

missionary a person who goes abroad to teach and spread (usually the Christian) religion

mistress a woman who is having a sexual relationship with a man she is not married to

moor a wide, open, often high area of land, covered with rough grass and bushes

nursemaid a woman employed to take care of babies and children

porridge a cooked breakfast cereal, eaten hot

prayer speaking to God; prayers a religious meeting in a school

rat an animal like a large mouse; calling a person a rat can be an insult

reveal to show something that was hidden or secret

rule *(n)* a fixed instruction that must be obeyed, e.g. as in a school

seize to take hold of quickly

servant someone employed to do work in a house

slate a piece of flat stone used for writing on

spirit the soul, the part of us which Christians believe does not die; sometimes, a ghost

stern *(adj)* unsmiling, a little angry

stocking a covering for girls' and women's legs

surname a family or last name

tell fortunes to say what will happen to someone in the future

tray a flat board for carrying cups and plates

tuberculosis a serious disease of the lungs which used to be fatal

typhus fever a fever easily passed from one person to another

vicar a priest in the Church of England